OSPREY MILITARY

CAMPAIGN SERIES   5

ARDENNES 1944

GENERAL EDITOR DAVID G. CHANDLER

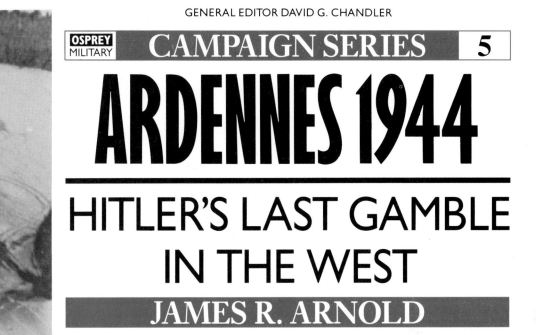

OSPREY MILITARY

CAMPAIGN SERIES 5

ARDENNES 1944

HITLER'S LAST GAMBLE IN THE WEST

JAMES R. ARNOLD

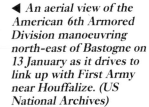

◀ *An aerial view of the American 6th Armored Division manoeuvring north-east of Bastogne on 13 January as it drives to link up with First Army near Houffalize. (US National Archives)*

▼ *Generalfeldmarschall Gerd von Rundstedt (on Hitler's left) was nominally in command of the entire Western Front. In reality he was more a figurehead. However, Allied intelligence believed that his conservative style dominated German planning, overlooking the vital fact that Hitler dominated all. Hitler did not consult him over Ardennes planning issues. Von Rundstedt realized that 'the available forces were far too small for such an extremely ambitious plan'. When he learned of Hitler's plan he scoffed: 'Antwerp? If we should reach the Meuse we should go down on our knees and thank God!' (US National Archives)*

Acknowledgements
Numerous people contributed to the completion of this book. My wife, Roberta Wiener, edited the manuscript and served as picture researcher, helping locate and select the photographs that appear in this book. Randy Hackenburg of the US Army Military History Institute, Carlisle, Pennsylvania, and the staff of the Still Pictures Branch, National Archives in Washington, DC, were most helpful in guiding us through their tremendous photograph collections. My friends at the Military Archive & Research Services in Lincolnshire kindly donated several prints from their collection. Photographers Robert C. Arnold and Ron Hyatt travelled to the various archives and reproduced the photographs at a moment's notice when time was of the essence. The reference librarians, most especially Ben Ritter, at Handley Library in Winchester, Virginia, processed my long list of interlibrary loan requests. I thank you all.

J.R.A.

For a catalogue of all books published by Osprey Military, please write to:

The Marketing Manager,
Consumer Catalogue Department, Osprey Publishing Ltd,
59 Grosvenor Street, London W1X 9DA.

First published in 1990 by Osprey Publishing Ltd, 59 Grosvenor Street, London W1X 9DA.

Produced by DAG Publications Ltd for Osprey Publishing Ltd.
Colour bird's eye view illustrations by Cilla Eurich.

British Library Cataloguing in Publication Data
Arnold, James R., *1952–*
Ardennes 1944: Hitler's last gamble in the West. – (Osprey campaign series; v.5).
1. World War 2. Battle of the Ardennes, 1944
I. Title
940.5421
ISBN 0-85045-959-1

Cartography by Micromap.
Wargaming Ardennes 1944 by Richard Marsh.
Wargames consultant Duncan Macfarlane.
Typeset by Typesetters (Birmingham) Ltd, Warley.
Mono camerawork by M&E Reproductions, North Fambridge, Essex.
Printed and bound in Hong Kong.

CONTENTS

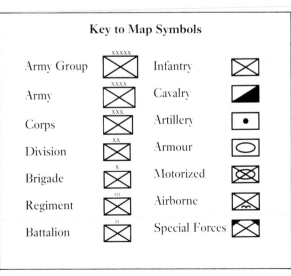

Key to Map Symbols

Army Group		Infantry	
Army		Cavalry	
Corps		Artillery	
Division		Armour	
Brigade		Motorized	
Regiment		Airborne	
Battalion		Special Forces	

BACKGROUND TO CRISIS: THE PLAN IS BORN

The Normandy breakout and subsequent blitz-krieg across north-western Europe ended when the Allies confronted the concrete fortifications of the West Wall along the German border. Henceforth, each tactical event dramatically altered Allied high command confidence in the war's outcome. The US 12th Army Group commander, Lieutenant General Omar Bradley, recalls that in early September 1944 – following the glory days of the pursuit across France – most generals believed victory was imminent. The amazing revitalization of the German Army in October, what the Germans called 'the Miracle of the West', stabilized the front and sobered many. Then, the bloody failure of the November offensive to crack the West Wall plunged Eisenhower and his staff into depressed planning for a winter stalemate. Yet when intelligence officers sifted through November results they decided matters were not so bleak. They believed that continuous Allied pressure was inflicting 9,000 German casualties per day, a manpower drain of five divisions per week. Resurgent optimism swept from Supreme Headquarters Allied Expeditionary Force (SHAEF) downward. Bradley's G-2 (Intelligence) wrote: 'the breaking point may develop suddenly and without warning.' Montgomery's G-2 echoed this belief: 'The enemy is in a bad way . . . he cannot stage a major offensive operation.'

This optimism hid a worsening schism within the Allied camp. Montgomery unrelentingly continued his campaign to boot Eisenhower upstairs so he could be replaced by one supreme land general, namely himself. The Field Marshal believed that all offensive operations south of the Ardennes should be halted so that all resources could be massed north of there in support of a single, 'full-blooded' thrust into the Ruhr. American generals, led by Bradley and Patton, bitterly resisted Montgomery's plan. Regardless of its

military merit – and the Americans believed that Montgomery had repeatedly demonstrated his incapacity to direct bold offensive movements – it placed American units in a subordinate role while reserving to the British the prestige of leading the final assault into Germany. Given that the number of American divisions in northern Europe greatly exceeded the number of British and Commonwealth divisions (42 to 19 at the height of the Ardennes offensive), Montgomery's plan was politically impossible. Yet he continued to advance it at all opportunities, forcing Eisenhower into one of the many unfortunate compromises in which he specialized. Eisenhower decreed that the Allies would close up on the Rhine by attacking on both sides of the Ardennes and then decide what to do. The middle, in the Ardennes itself – an area believed unproductive for either Allied or German offensive action – would be thinly held by battered veteran divisions and recently arrived green divisions.

As early as 19 August, Adolf Hitler began laying the groundwork for what would become the Ardennes offensive. It was remarkable strategic effrontery to consider a major offensive even as the German Army was in the midst of its most punishing losses in five years of war: August saw it lose nearly half a million men, raising the five-year total to some 3.3 million casualties. Yet with the front collapsing, and major units such as the Panzer Lehr Division reduced to a handful of men and five tanks, he ordered units assembled and held in reserve for a decisive counterstroke. In the German view, a successful attack in the East might eliminate 20-30 Russian divisions, but this would hardly alter the strategic situation. Similar results in the West would have decisive impact.

Henceforth, Hitler's strategy called for holding firm on all fronts until offensive preparations were complete. He believed that the British and Americans would be forced to halt after outrunning their supplies. Then the defenders could regroup behind the formidable West Wall fortifications. It was an intuitive conclusion that proved accurate. Furthermore, Hitler believed that the Allied coalition was an unnatural grouping of rival interests. A solid blow would cause the coalition to collapse. Hitler patterned his beliefs on Frederick the Great's experience at the end of the Seven Years War – when, by stubbornly continuing the war against all advice, Fredrick had outlasted the coalition ranked against him. Hitler believed he could do the same. In his view, the key was offensive action. By attacking he would prove to the Western allies that Germany could not be conquered.

On 16 September, Hitler interrupted a staff meeting to announce his 'momentous decision . . . to go over to the counterattack! Here, out of the Ardennes, with the objective – Antwerp!' Such a thrust would sever the American and British armies and lead to 'another Dunkirk'. The attack would take place in bad weather to neutralize the overwhelming Allied air superiority. Western countermeasures would be slow, Hitler believed, because of the Allies' need to coordinate plans. Therefore, German tanks should be able to bounce the River Meuse before Allied reserves entered the fray. Furthermore, Hitler had no

respect for the American fighting man. He felt sure that a surprise blitzkreig assault, backed by special commando units to spread confusion and terror, and pursued ruthlessly, would quickly crack the American line in the Ardennes.

▼ *From the east the Russians closed in on the borders of the Reich. Ignoring the advice of Guderian and others, Hitler chose to send reinforcements west. In November and December, 2,277 new armoured fighting vehicles went west and only 919 went east. This left German lines in the east thinly* *stretched, with infantry forced to fend for themselves against Russian tanks. Here soldiers armed with two stick-grenades, on front lip of foxhole, wait as a Russian T-34 comes into view from the left. (Wood Collection, US Army Military History Institute)*

▶ *By late 1944, Bradley was using the Ardennes sector to refit battered units. To defend the long front, most battalions had to employ some of their specialist troops such as mortar men, gunners and anti-tank company men, as riflemen. Patton noted in his diary in early December that the theatre-wide shortage of infantry replacements meant 'we are stretched pretty thin'. Here GIs line up for a movie at the quiet backwater town of Malmédy, five days before the German counter-offensive begins. (US National Archives)*

THE OPPOSING FORCES

American Infantry

Pre-war American planners designed the infantry division for mobility rather than power. It had an authorized strength of 14,253, divided into three regiments of three battalions with three rifle companies each. The division's core strength resided in its 27 rifle companies which totalled, along with headquarters personnel, 5,211 officers and men. The balance of the division's manpower was in support units. Experience showed that the divisional structure lacked enough riflemen for sustained combat and thus a unit's striking edge quickly dulled in the furnace of battle.

Like all other armies, the display of firepower during the First World War changed American infantry doctrine to emphasize fire and man-oeuvre. On the squad and platoon level this required aggressive, intelligent action. Yet the US Army filled its combat infantry ranks with the uneducated, unskilled, and unenthusiastic re-cruits, leaving the better quality recruits for the technical branches. Post-war studies found that only fifteen percent of riflemen in average units ever fired a shot during combat. In élite formations such as the paratroopers, the percentage doubled.

▼ *Compared with his opponent, the GI was a superior marksman and fired the best rifle of the war, the M1 Garand semi-automatic. The standard German rifles were bolt-action. Both sides employed comparable light machine-guns. The Americans carried two First World War vintage weapons: a Browning automatic rifle, one per squad; and a heavy .50-calibre water-cooled machine-gun, a weapon type the Germans had abandoned. Here 30th Division GIs relax behind the front on 16 December. They would soon be fighting Peiper. The seated figure has a BAR in his right hand and an M1 in his left, plus .50-calibre machine-gun bullets draped across his shoulders. (US Army Military History Institute)*

▶ *Most defenders in the Ardennes had too few bazookas and were short of ammunition. Typical of the battle, on 17 December a platoon facing five Tiger tanks on a key trail leading to Rocherath-Krinkelt had three rounds of bazooka ammunition. Here bazooka instruction is carried out against a knocked out Mark IV. (US Army Military History Institute)*

▲ Two-thirds of an infantry division's strength was in support units. According to Patton: '92% of all casualties occur in the infantry rifle companies, and that when the infantry division has lost 4,000 men, it has practically no riflemen left.' The 28th Infantry Division, holding the central Ardennes sector, had lost 6,100 men in the Huertgen Forest. The American Army was also officer heavy; officers represented 7 per cent of manpower, while the German percentage was 2.86. Shown here are some of the few at the sharp end: an infantry-tank team of the 4th Armored Division near Bastogne. (Charles B. MacDonald Collection, US Army Military History Institute)

All this meant that American infantry lacked aggressiveness in the attack, a characteristic that manifested itself during the counterattack phase of the Battle of the Bulge.

In defence, the GI could more than hold his own against his generally poorly trained counterparts who filled the German ranks. When confronting hostile armour, as would be the case during the critical first days of the coming battle, the infantry suffered a crippling lack of effective anti-tank weapons. As far back as 1943 in Sicily, the GIs had found that their standard hand-held 2.36in rocket launcher, the bazooka, failed against late-model panzers. Yet the Ordnance Department did not develop and supply an alternative.

In theory each US infantry regiment relied on its anti-tank company with six 57mm anti-tank guns. This was a pitiful, obsolete weapon. Sim-

US infantryman, armed with an M1 carbine.

ilarly, the GIs were at a qualitative disadvantage with their close-support artillery. Each regiment had a cannon company comprising six towed, short-barrelled 105mm howitzers. They simply lacked the mobility, particularly in the Ardennes mud and snow, to be useful. In contrast, the Germans had developed a special category of weapon to assist their attacking infantry through the fire zone: self-propelled 75mm assault guns.

The saving weapon for the American infantry was undoubtedly the artillery. The divisional artillery had three twelve-piece 105mm howitzer battalions and one twelve-piece 155mm battalion. Because the mechanics of serving an artillery piece are similar to training exercises – the men do the same thing in training as in combat, laying fire on targets they do not see – green artillery crews performed about as well as veterans. Thus the inexperienced divisions fighting in the Ardennes could expect good artillery support. Since 1942 the Germans had looked down on the American infantry but praised its artillery. Along the entire Ardennes front the defenders employed 228 artillery pieces in 13 general support battalions, and 276 pieces organic to the division. Across the lines the Germans massed some 1,900 artillery and rocket tubes.

In refutation of pre-war doctrine, by 1944 each American infantry division had an attached tank battalion with a 13-tank light company and three medium companies with 53 tanks. When confronted by charging panzers, the mediums in the attached battalions seemed to lack the willingness to support the infantry in the front line. This is understandable given the great qualitative superiority of the German tanks.

The picture that emerges of the standard 1944 US infantry division is not a happy one. Fallacious doctrine had led to poor organizational structure. Worse, in the vital area of anti-tank combat, the men had obsolete weapons. The Ardennes has been called the American Army's 'nursery and the old folk's home'. Here veteran formations absorbed thousands of 'reinforcements' – for psychological reasons the brass had decreed that the former term 'replacements' no longer be used – and were held together by a hard cadre of survivors. The new divisions were untested, yet

▶ The standard American anti-tank weapon was the obsolete 57mm gun. It could stop Mark IVs and light armour but was next to useless against heavier panzers. For years the Germans and Russians had used more powerful 75mm or larger guns for anti-tank weapons. Somehow the American Army, having the world's largest industrial base to draw on, could not provide its infantry with an adequate tank-killing weapon. Men of the 84th Division man a 57mm anti-tank gun in a snow-storm on 4 January. (US National Archives)

▶ US gunners enjoyed the advantage of advanced communications and fire control equipment, which allowed them to engage new targets rapidly. They had perfected the deadly 'TOT' (time on target) tactic that permitted multiple batteries to fire on selected targets for designated periods of time. The resultant volume of fire accurately delivered to a small area awed the Germans. Here a 105mm self-propelled howitzer of Battery C, 274 Field Artillery Battalion fires a mission on 1 January near Bastogne. (US National Archives)

▶ The basis for attaching a tank battalion to the infantry was to provide slugging power for frontal attacks; however, including light tanks, a design made especially for exploitation and pursuit, made no sense. Once or twice during the Ardennes battle the light companies caught German infantry in the open. Otherwise they proved useless. (US National Archives)

▲ The infantry division had an attached tank destroyer (TD) battalion. Pre-war planners believed that tanks would avoid combat with opposing tanks. Experience showed that tanks were the most effective tank killers. The standard M10 featured a 3in high-velocity gun in an open turret (to save weight and increase mobility) mounted on a Sherman chassis. The need to upgrade became apparent, so that by 1944 some were redesigned to accommodate a 90mm gun. Other models in the Ardennes included the M18 with a 76mm gun in an open turret on a light tank chassis. The design effort to unite mobility and gun power at the expense of armour proved a failure. Here a TD provides support to dug-in infantry. (US National Archives)

▶ German tank guns outranged and had higher muzzle velocity than the Sherman's short 75mm gun. The Sherman's gun could penetrate neither the Mark V Panther's nor the Mark VI Tiger's frontal armour, while its own frontal armour could not withstand the German tank and anti-tank guns. The Sherman's only viable tactic was to work for a side or rear shot. During the Ardennes campaign, muddy conditions often restricted combat to the road, thus eliminating the theoretical American counter. In any event, to take out a Panther or Tiger usually required the expenditure of several Shermans, a fact, Bradley noted, that 'offered little comfort to the crews who were forced to expend themselves'. A Tiger's rounds have twice penetrated this Sherman, killing driver and setting tank afire. (US National Archives)

◀ In 1942 the standard American tank, the 33-tonne M4 General Sherman, had entered combat with the British Eighth Army. It proved a good match for the then current German main battle tank, the Mark IV. While Germany and Russia, with inferior industrial bases, managed annually to upgrade tank design, American design stood frozen in time. What worked in 1942 was badly obsolete in 1944. A 3rd Armored Division Sherman guards the road near Manhay. (US National Archives)

Bradley and others knew that green divisions almost invariably failed in Europe in their first battle and took heavy losses while doing so.

American Armour

US armoured divisions typically had three battalions with 177 medium tanks, 77 light tanks equipped with the useless 37mm gun, a self-propelled tank destroyer battalion, three self-propelled medium artillery battalions and three so-called armoured infantry battalions. In fact, once the latter dismounted from their half-tracks, they fought in just the same way as other infantry. The division divided into three combat commands. Tank crews in the armoured divisions consistently showed a willingness to engage enemy tanks. Their Shermans were slightly superior to the German Mark IVs. Against the heavier panzers, they fought at an enormous disadvantage.

Given the American technical inferiority, it is not surprising that nearly every reported German tank was a 'Tiger' and every anti-tank gun an '88'. What surprises across time is the American willingness to fight when they well understood the enemy advantages. In Normandy and during the pursuit across France, the Shermans relied upon superior numbers and bountiful air support to beat the panzers. On 16 December, VIII Corps had 242 Shermans and 182 self-propelled TDs to face about 1,000 German tanks and assault guns, in weather conditions that kept most aircraft grounded.

Given the American problems, it is fortunate that their German counterparts also suffered severe deficiencies.

German Infantry

Heavy losses forced the Germans to restructure their infantry divisions in 1944. To appeal for the patriotic defence of the Fatherland, Hitler created the Volksgrenadier Division (VGD). Formerly this title had to be won in battle. Under new decrees, young recruits, 16- and 17-year-olds in the VGD, and younger 'volunteers' in the SS, joined older men now liable for service to fill the ranks of the refitting formations designated for the Ardennes

▲*The German light machine-gun had such a high rate of fire that soldiers called it the 'Hitler-Sage' (Hitler's Saw). Captured film shows machine-gunner (in middle) on 17 December. (US National Archives)*

attack. Many more soldiers came from rear area comb-outs and Luftwaffe and Navy personnel. While their morale remained high – only five soldiers deserted along the entire Western front in the first twelve days of December – they had been hastily trained and knew little of infantry tactics. They tended to advance in clumps, herded forward by veteran NCOs and officers and suffered horrible losses to automatic weapons and artillery fire. Authorized manpower declined from just over 17,000 in the old style divisions to 12,769, divided into three regiments of two battalions each. An élite fusilier battalion gave the division an additional manoeuvre element.

Accompanying the decline in German manpower was an increase in individual firepower. The machine pistol, lavishly distributed to the Volksgrenadiers, proved very successful, particularly when wielded by each regiment's special assault company. The Germans also had what an Ameri-

German Volksgrenadier, armed with Panzerfaust and a Soviet PPSh41 submachine-gun.

▲ *Among various machine-pistols was the famous Schmeisser, whose high cyclic rate of fire made a 'b-r-r-r-r-p' sound, thus winning the name 'burp gun' to the GIs. In spite of the fact that a German division contained 1,200 fewer infantrymen than an American infantry division, the German wealth of automatic weapons gave them superior firepower. Here captured film shows a cyclist delivering a message to infantry riding on the rear of a panzer during the advance. Note the man standing on the left carries a captured Sten gun. (US National Archives)*

can paratroop general called 'the best hand-carried anti-tank weapon of the war', the one-shot Panzerfaust rocket launcher.

Infantry division artillery allocations were similar to those of the Americans. However, most artillery still relied upon horse-drawn transport, a fact that made the artillery slow to displace forward to support the advance and led to tremendous, momentum-numbing traffic jams along the German rear. Higher command echelons had nine

Volksartillerie corps ranging in number of guns from 50 to 100. They included many captured foreign weapons, thus greatly complicating ammunition supply. High command also directed seven new Volkswerfer brigades equipped with rocket-firing Nebelwerfers. Once the spearhead formations outstripped the range of the horse-drawn tube artillery, they relied upon the fully motorized rocket brigades for artillery support. Typically, Goering promised massive Luftwaffe

▶ *The Germans distributed their version of the rocket launcher, the panzerfaust, in lavish numbers. They were easily carried in a shoulder sling that allowed the individual to operate other weapons. The commander of the 82nd Airborne Division noted that his men only acquired an adequate anti-tank weapon after it captured numerous panzerfausts. An anti-tank gunner of the 26th VGD drew this sketch showing his unit advancing near Bastogne on 20 December. The front two marching soldiers are carrying panzerfausts. (Charles B. MacDonald Collection, US Army Military History Institute)*

▶ *German rocket brigades could deliver terrifying saturation fire. The GIs called them 'screaming meemies' because of the sound an incoming rocket made. Fully motorized Nebelwerfer units allowed the Germans to bring forward firepower to support the offensive. They were also used to beef up special assault units. SS Panzer divisions had an attached Nebelwerfer battalion, an extra tank or panzerjaeger battalion, and a heavy 170mm artillery battery. (Military Archive & Research Services)*

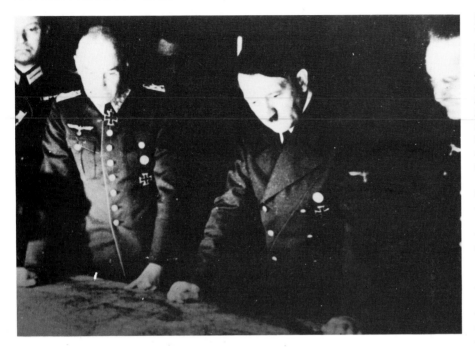

▲ *By autumn 1944, Adolf Hitler exercised total control over the German military. Von Manteuffel recalls that Hitler never possessed 'the form of concentration used by our General Staff officers. He just didn't have the mental faculties to consider any plan up to the minutest details.' Hitler regarded his own military leadership as 'A matter of intellect, tenacity and nerves of steel! Will power was all!'*

Hitler distanced himself from the professional Prussian staff officers and surrounded himself with sycophants. He was thus ignorant of, and divorced from, the most basic principles of war. The 20 July failed assassination attempt took a heavy physical and psychological toll and made him ever more suspicious of the officer corps: 'He came into the map room bent and shuffling. His glassy eyes

gave a sign of recognition only to those who stood closest to him.' He slumped into his chair 'bent almost double with his head sunk between his shoulders'. Pointing to the map, his hand trembled. 'On the slightest occasion he would demand shrilly that "the guilty" be hunted down.' He was the principal German strategist for the Ardennes offensive. (Personality Pictures Library)

▶ *Generalfeldmarschall Walter Model was one of the architects of the 'Miracle of the West'. Apprised in late October of the pending offensive, he responded: 'This plan hasn't got a damned leg to stand on.' He unsuccessfully advanced a more practical, limited alternative, the so-called 'small solution'. He commanded Army Group B, comprising the armies taking part in the Ardennes offensive. Model's attack order read: 'We will not disappoint the Führer and the Fatherland, who created the sword of retribution. Forward in the spirit of Leuthen!' (Military Archive & Research Services)*

Generaloberst Alfred Jodl (not shown) was foremost among Hitler's toadies in the planning of the Ardennes offensive. As chief of the OKW operations staff, he had lived in Hitler's presence for years. Isolated and out of touch, he assumed planning direction for the counter-offensive. The Ardennes operation was the first time in six years of war that OKW took direct control of a major offensive. Jodl saw this as his great opportunity. His inability to stand up to Hitler, coupled with his own and his staff's inexperience, led to many planning blunders. When von Manteuffel tried to advance his opinions on how to conduct the offensive on 3 November, Jodl kept interrupting by shouting: 'That is an order of the Führer! Nothing is to change – all irrevocable!' (US National
◀ *Archives)*

▲General der Panzertruppen Hasso von Manteuffel, the commander of Fifth Panzer Army, was the kind of aggressive, brainy leader who earned worldwide military respect for the 'Prussian tradition'. A mere battalion commander during the invasion of Russia in 1941, he performed with such distinction that he caught the eye of Hitler himself. At a time when few officers dared argue with the Führer, von Manteuffel managed to persuade Hitler about significant assault tactics, yet he worried that years of Hitler's operational control had 'brought about the death of the German art of flexible command'. Liddell Hart called him 'a master of the art of mobility and surprise'. Von Manteuffel's attack order: 'Forward, march, march! In remembrance of our dead comrades, and therefore on their order, and in remembrance of the tradition of our proud Wehrmacht!' (Military Archive & Research Services)

◀ Generaloberst Josef 'Sepp' Dietrich was a long-time Hitler crony, hand-picked to command Sixth Panzer Army. Given the best equipment and all the SS forces, his task was to lead the breakthrough. Of limited ability, he had little impact on the battle. His chief of staff made most army-level decisions. (US National Archives)

▼*Sturmgeschutz III Ausf G of Skorzeny's 150th Panzer Brigade.*

◀ *For the assault, infantry relied increasingly on self-propelled assault guns to escort them through the fire zone. Their battle drill emphasized use of these weapons. Afterwards, commanders blamed them when infantry assaults failed. Assigned 18 to a division, as well as organized into separate support detachments, these weapons also gave the German infantry an effective anti-tank weapon. There was a shortage of these weapons: the entire Seventh Army had only 30. Here infantry ride an assault gun as it attacks on 17 December. (US National Archives)*

support; but, except for one last spectacular day when the Luftwaffe performed its death flight – the Great Blow – the Luftwaffe exerted little influence on ground combat.

The panzergrenadier (PG) and parachute divisions retained their structure and so still had nine infantry battalions. The PG divisions resembled American infantry divisions. They were fully motorized and had organic medium tank and TD

battalions. The two parachute divisions kept their name as an honorific, for they were no longer the élite units of past campaigns.

German Armour

German panzer and SS panzer divisions had one panzer regiment and two panzergrenadier regiments. The divisions averaged 90 to 100 medium

▶ *Even this late in the war, German tank crews maintained a high standard of driving, firing and radio signal functions. According to some experts, the latest model Panther, equipped with infra-red night sight optics, remained the world's best tank through the early 1950s. In December 1944, it far outclassed its American opponents. (US National Archives)*

▼*Panzerkampfwagen VI Tiger II Ausf B of Panzer Abteilung 501.*

tanks. Each type of division had a self-propelled anti-tank battalion. Equivalent to the American armoured infantry, the panzergrenadiers lacked their American counterparts' mobility. Only one-quarter of them rode half-tracks, and material shortages reduced the balance to riding a motley collection of captured vehicles reflecting the flow and ebb of German fortunes since the beginning of the war. The army PG regiments had two battalions each, the SS three. Of the three artillery battalions assigned to the Army divisions, only one was self-propelled. In the SS, one in four was self-propelled. Since the plan for the Ardennes offensive called for the SS to carry the main effort, each SS panzer division had attached units to provide enhanced firepower.

The two panzer battalions in the panzer regiment provided the power for a blitzkreig. Generally, one battalion comprised the 'workhorse' tank, the 75mm gun-armed, 27-tonne Mark IV. It was vulnerable to bazookas and other American anti-tank weapons. The other battalion employed the 43-tonne Mark V or Panther. The Panther had a long 75mm gun – 70 calibres larger than the Sherman's short 75mm gun – that was decisively superior in range and muzzle velocity to American

tanks. It had considerably thicker armour and better cross-country mobility in mud and snow.

Even more formidable appearing was the Mark VI or Tiger tank. Weighing 63 tonnes, armed with the deadly 88mm gun, it carried enough armour to render its front and sides all but invulnerable. The newest model, the Royal, or King, Tiger, weighed 68 tonnes – the heaviest operational tank of the war – and had turret armour more than seven inches thick. Its high-velocity, long 88mm gun fired a 22-pound shell capable of destroying a Sherman at a half mile range. Fortunately for the Americans, the closed terrain and frequently poor visibility partially negated the German tank gun range superiority.

Hitler ordered the Tigers distributed in independent formations, generally company and battalion size, and used to beef up important attacks. About 45 Royal Tigers and 200 Tigers participated in the Ardennes offensive. Dietrich's Sixth Panzer Army received 21 experimental Jagdtigers, a 82-tonne panzerjaeger with the huge 128mm gun, a weapon that had been the mainstay of German anti-aircraft defence. Overall the Germans brought about 1,000 tanks or tank-type vehicles to the opening assault.

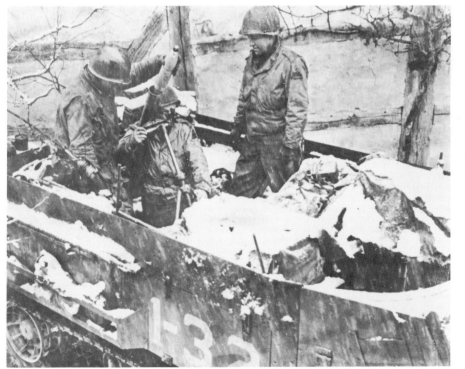

◀ *Weather determined the offensive's timing. 'Führer weather' featuring rain, fog and snow would ground Allied air power. Here a 2nd Armored Division mortar carrier fires during a blizzard in preparation for a counterattack at the tip of the Bulge. (US Army Military History Institute)*

▶ *Lieutenant General Omar Bradley, here decorating Lieutenant General Courtney Hodges after the battle, commanded the mostly American 12th Army Group. Beneath his quiet exterior he was an aggressive leader. Frustration over Eisenhower's seeming preference for British strategies consumed his headquarters. Bradley viewed the Ardennes sector as 'a calculated risk'; the German offensive greatly surprised him. He responded with soldierly skill but was dismayed when Montgomery assumed command of American forces north of the breakthrough. Hodges commanded the US First Army, the army hit by the German offensive. Slow to appreciate German intentions, his limited grand-tactical skills were exhausted by the first days. (US Army Military History Institute)*

▶ *General Dwight Eisenhower was Supreme Allied Commander in ' Europe. While nearly everyone liked the amiable 'Ike,' neither his American nor his British subordinates respected his military prowess. The Anglo-American competition for scarce resources plagued his headquarters, forcing him to make many decisions on a political rather than a military basis. The Ardennes offensive witnessed his finest hour as military leader. Here Ike tours Bastogne with Bradley (left) and Patton. Lieutenant General George Patton commanded US Third Army south of the bulge*

and, alone among top Allied generals, he worried about a German Ardennes attack. However, absorbed with his own pending

offensive, he unwillingly recognized the moment when it came. Once convinced, he rapidly sent his army to attack the German flank.

Undoubtedly he was the most aggressive Allied army commander and the one most respected by the Germans. (US National Archives)

▲ Left to right:
Lieutenant General
George Patton,
commanding officer of the
US Third Army; General
Dwight D. Eisenhower,
Supreme Commander,
Allied Forces Europe; and
Lieutenant General Omar
Bradley, commanding
officer of the US First
Army.

Eastern front armoured combat featured tremendous armour concentrations on a narrow front. In the west, Allied air superiority prohibited these tactics. Fighter-bombers ('Jabos' in German army slang) dominated mechanized ground combat. Lacking an effective counter, Hitler promised poor weather conditions that would ground the Allied air forces. What passes for intuition was actually based on the careful analysis of long range weather reports by his meteorological expert Dr Karl Recknagel.

In the early months of autumn 1944, U-boats deposited weather teams around the Arctic Circle. There they fought an amazing cat and mouse

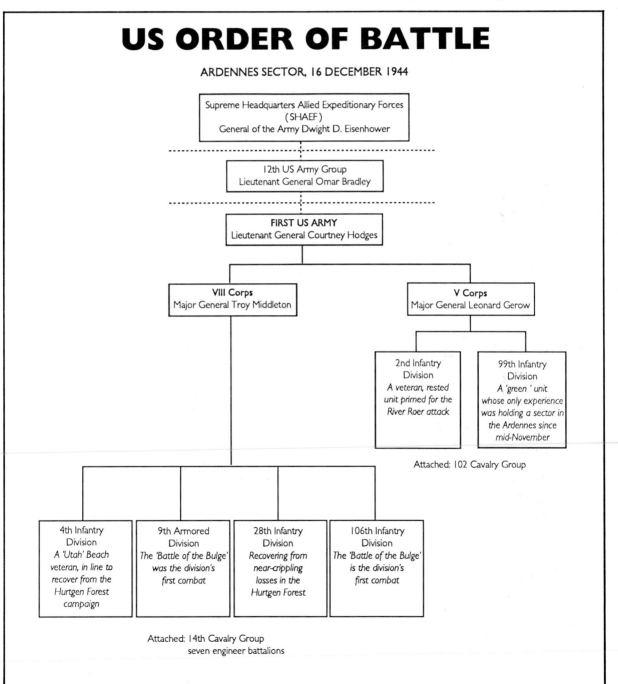

US ORDER OF BATTLE

ARDENNES SECTOR, 16 DECEMBER 1944

Supreme Headquarters Allied Expeditionary Forces
(SHAEF)
General of the Army Dwight D. Eisenhower

12th US Army Group
Lieutenant General Omar Bradley

FIRST US ARMY
Lieutenant General Courtney Hodges

VIII Corps
Major General Troy Middleton

V Corps
Major General Leonard Gerow

2nd Infantry
Division
A veteran, rested unit primed for the River Roer attack

99th Infantry
Division
A 'green' unit whose only experience was holding a sector in the Ardennes since mid-November

Attached: 102 Cavalry Group

4th Infantry
Division
A 'Utah' Beach veteran, in line to recover from the Hurtgen Forest campaign

9th Armored
Division
The 'Battle of the Bulge' was the division's first combat

28th Infantry
Division
Recovering from near-crippling losses in the Hurtgen Forest

106th Infantry
Division
The 'Battle of the Bulge' is the division's first combat

Attached: 14th Cavalry Group
seven engineer battalions

combat against Allied patrols sent to ferret out their secret radio stations. One team, sent to the Spitzbergen area, narrowly avoided British destroyers which had been alerted by Ultra intercepts to expect their landing. They established a weather station that continued in operation four months after the Wehrmacht's capitulation, the last German unit to surrender in the war. In Berlin, Recknagel analyzed these remote reports and predicted that the last two weeks of December would see rain, fog and heavy snow. He said that these conditions would begin on 16 December, a date German planners accepted for beginning the attack.

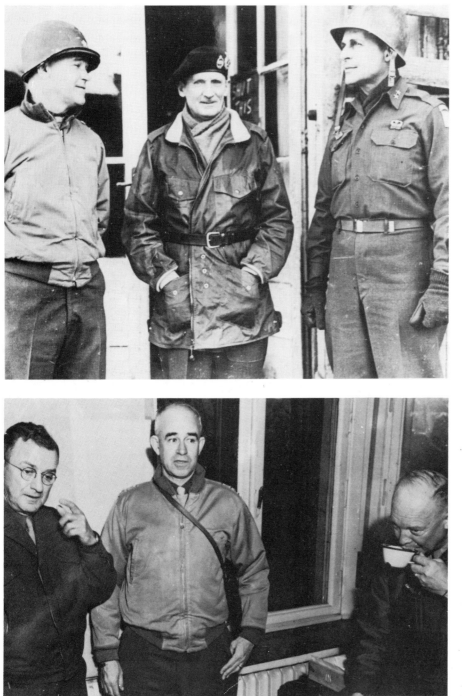

◄ *Field Marshal Sir Bernard Montgomery commanded 21st Army Group, comprising all British and dominion as well as many American formations. A self-described Great Captain, the near total depletion of British manpower reserves thwarted his offensive concepts. Fortune beckoned when he took over command of American units north of the Bulge. He promptly ran foul of American doctrine and sensibilities. Most American generals disliked the pompous Monty, yet those who worked closest with him respected his abilities. He is seen here with two of his American subordinates; Collins on left and Ridgeway. (US National Archives)*

◄ *Major General Troy Middleton (left) commanded VIII Corps where the German blow fell. A First World War veteran, he was described by Marshall as 'the outstanding infantry regimental commander' on the French battlefield. Both Bradley (right) and Eisenhower (far right) sought him for corps command. Patton wrote that Middleton acquitted himself 'exceptionally well' during the campaign. Yet his complacency before the attack, failure to patrol and failure to fortify, proved costly. (US Army Military History Institute)*

Deception and Intelligence

Hitler believed that the German enciphering system for wireless communications was absolutely secure. It relied upon an ingenious machine known as Enigma, and by 1944 the Allies routinely decoded nearly all of its transmissions. The Germans had begun to realize that somehow the Western Allies had penetrated their secrets. Confident that Enigma was uncrackable, Hitler attributed the leaks to spies and traitors. However, to prevent exposure of the coming offensive, he forbade all electronic transmission of plans connected with it. Instead, officer couriers – escorted by Gestapo agents – hand-delivered all communications. Unbeknown to the Allies, their most dependable source of intelligence would have little relevance for the coming attack.

The Germans took several other steps to hide their intentions. In a stroke of brilliance, Hitler assigned a deceptive, defensive sounding codename: 'Wacht am Rhein' (Watch on the Rhine). Most movement orders designed to mass troops for the attack began with the words 'in preparation for the anticipated enemy offensive'. Oberkommando der Wehrmacht (OKW) planners intentionally exposed one of the two assault armies, Sixth Panzer, to Allied aerial reconnaissance in the Cologne area, where it seemed poised to counterattack the American drive on the Rhine. Just three days before the attack it moved into its real staging area. The other assault army, Fifth Panzer, took over the defensive fighting near Aachen as cover for its offensive deployment. It then withdrew from the defensive fighting, seemingly to refit, as its commander planned the attack while hiding under the name 'Military Police Command for Special Assignment'. This labyrinth of deception confounded Allied intelligence officers.

The Germans achieved amazing success in massing their forces under skies thoroughly dominated by enemy aircraft. Key to this success was the Reichsbahn (the German State Railway). Rail lines leading to the Eifel (the German extension of the Ardennes) had been located based on anticipated military needs for the First World War. Reinforced for the 1940 campaign, they again proved themselves a model of efficiency in 1944.

Trains hauling the vast store of supplies needed for the offensive moved only at night, hiding by day in tunnels or dispersing along rear-area marshalling yards. In November alone trains dumped 3,982 wagon-loads of supplies into assembly areas. Allied air power destroyed a mere four wagon-loads of fuel during the entire month.

So the secret build-up continued, bringing divisions from all over Hitler's empire. Ethnic Germans from border regions were sent to the rear lest they desert and reveal the plan. For the final massing at the front, staff officers orchestrated a three-day forward movement along prescribed staging lines. Three days before the attack they moved up no closer than twelve miles from the front; two days, six miles; the last day, two miles. It utilized time-tested methods dating back to the German offensives in the First World War. They moved only at night, hiding during the day in the Eifel forests, cooking only with smokeless charcoal fires in fear of the special security detachments who roamed in search of anyone violating camouflage discipline. The troops knew nothing of the

▼ *Germans operate an Enigma machine in France in 1940. (US National Archives)*

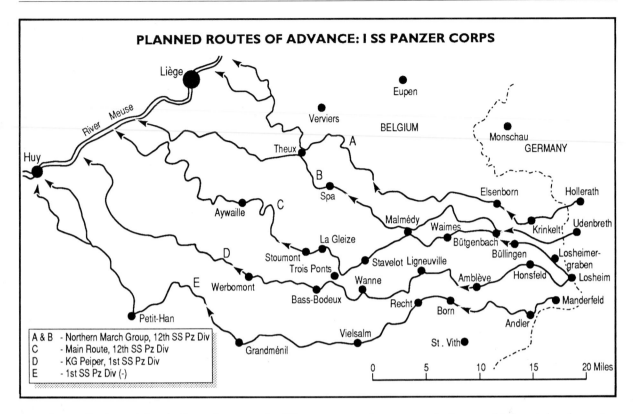

PLANNED ROUTES OF ADVANCE: I SS PANZER CORPS

A & B - Northern March Group, 12th SS Pz Div
C - Main Route, 12th SS Pz Div
D - KG Peiper, 1st SS Pz Div
E - 1st SS Pz Div (-)

assault until the night before the attack. The preparations were carried out with the brilliance for which the German General Staff was renowned – and yet the Americans had ample clues to detect the attack.

The main problem was that everyone believed the Germans were beaten. Beyond that, intelligence officers had grown too reliant on Enigma intercepts. These intercepts informed them of a westward shift of German fighters and of the creation of a large panzer reserve, but that was all. In the past, intercepts had specified when and where attacks would occur. Without such additional information, few believed the Germans were about to launch a major offensive. No one could explain Enigma intercepts of German requests for photo reconnaissance of the River Meuse crossing sites. Yet trusting that von Rundstedt commanded the German defence, and thus that the Germans would behave logically and husband their strength to counterattack the coming Allied offensive, few became alarmed.

The twin beliefs that the Germans were desperately short of resources and that von Rundstedt was in charge coloured the interpretation of aerial reconnaissance missions which sighted major movements around the Eifel and front-line reports of traffic noise. Intelligence officers decided that von Rundstedt was so hard-pressed that he was shuttling forces behind the Eifel to oppose American attacks. The train movements in the Cologne area were thought to support Sixth Panzer Army as it massed for its counterattack role. Had someone carefully examined the map, he might have seen that rail spur lines ran from the Cologne area to the Eifel.

In the final analysis, Allied intelligence officers possessed a core of hard information to deduce the German plan. They failed, and so the attackers achieved total surprise.

The Plan

Four American divisions held the 85-mile-long Ardennes front. American generals focused on the left-most flank where the 2nd Infantry Division prepared to attack the Roer dams. On the remainder of the front the Americans were content to remain passive. While the southern half of the line followed the course of the Rivers Our and

'Wacht am Rhein' - The German Plan

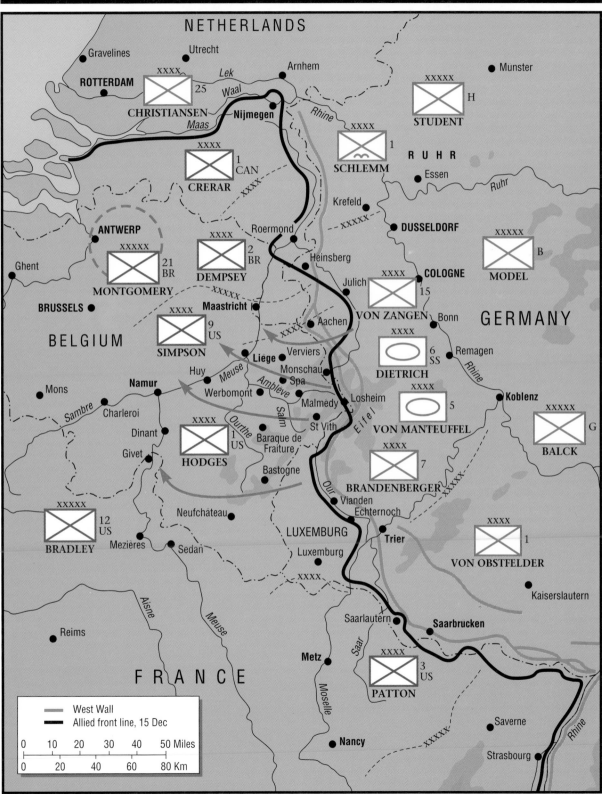

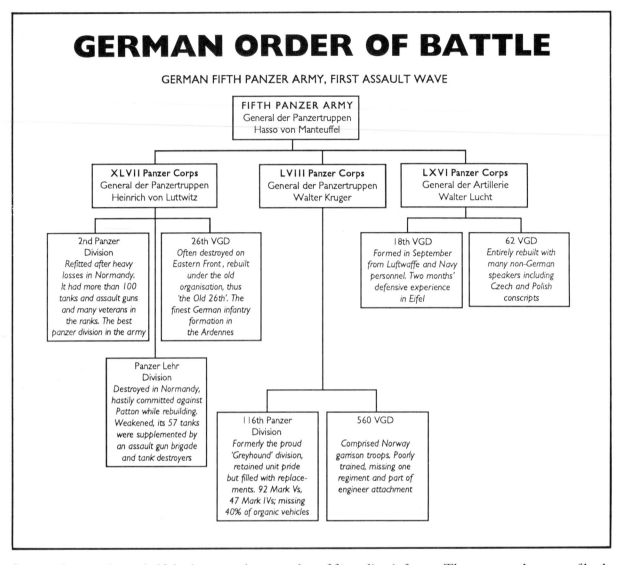

GERMAN ORDER OF BATTLE

GERMAN FIFTH PANZER ARMY, FIRST ASSAULT WAVE

FIFTH PANZER ARMY
General der Panzertruppen
Hasso von Manteuffel

XLVII Panzer Corps
General der Panzertruppen
Heinrich von Luttwitz

LVIII Panzer Corps
General der Panzertruppen
Walter Kruger

LXVI Panzer Corps
General der Artillerie
Walter Lucht

2nd Panzer Division
Refitted after heavy losses in Normandy. It had more than 100 tanks and assault guns and many veterans in the ranks. The best panzer division in the army

26th VGD
Often destroyed on Eastern Front, rebuilt under the old organisation, thus 'the Old 26th'. The finest German infantry formation in the Ardennes

18th VGD
Formed in September from Luftwaffe and Navy personnel. Two months' defensive experience in Eifel

62 VGD
Entirely rebuilt with many non-German speakers including Czech and Polish conscripts

Panzer Lehr Division
Destroyed in Normandy, hastily committed against Patton while rebuilding. Weakened, its 57 tanks were supplemented by an assault gun brigade and tank destroyers

116th Panzer Division
Formerly the proud 'Greyhound' division, retained unit pride but filled with replacements. 92 Mark Vs, 47 Mark IVs; missing 40% of organic vehicles

560 VGD
Comprised Norway garrison troops. Poorly trained, missing one regiment and part of engineer attachment

Sauer, the northern half had no such natural advantages. It represented the easternmost line reached by advancing forces back in the autumn. The line bulged forward to encompass the Schnee Eifel (Snow Plateau) where, back in September, the 4th Infantry Division had achieved a lodgement in the West Wall. This penetration led to no worthwhile objectives and so American planners turned elsewhere, but army and corps commanders mindlessly retained the salient. On 10 December, the green 106th Division took over the position.

Holding the entire Ardennes front with so few troops was a risk – Bradley and others later called it 'a calculated risk', but in fact it was no such thing – necessitated by the critical theatre-wide shortage of front-line infantry. There was a shortage of both divisions and manpower within divisions. Allied planners had badly miscalculated the rate of attrition 'at the sharp end'. They had allocated too few replacement infantry and too many replacement technical and service troops. Inept long-range planning was combined with heavy losses in the autumn. The unexpected onslaught of trench foot caused by slow delivery of poorly designed cold-weather footwear exacerbated the shortage. Consequently, Bradley had committed every division to the front line. Only the refitting 82nd and 101st Airborne Divisions remained in SHAEF reserve.

On 8 November, Bradley and Eisenhower visited Major General Troy Middleton, the com-

GERMAN ORDER OF BATTLE

ORDER OF BATTLE, GERMAN SEVENTH ARMY

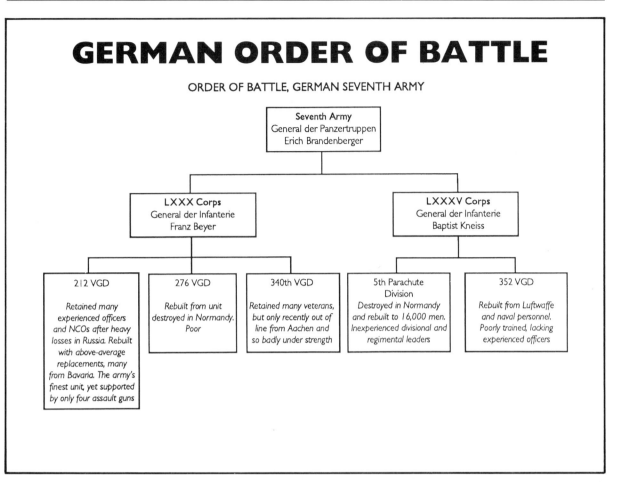

Seventh Army
General der Panzertruppen
Erich Brandenberger

LXXX Corps
General der Infanterie
Franz Beyer

LXXXV Corps
General der Infanterie
Baptist Kneiss

212 VGD

Retained many experienced officers and NCOs after heavy losses in Russia. Rebuilt with above-average replacements, many from Bavaria. The army's finest unit, yet supported by only four assault guns

276 VGD

Rebuilt from unit destroyed in Normandy. Poor

340th VGD

Retained many veterans, but only recently out of line from Aachen and so badly under strength

5th Parachute Division

Destroyed in Normandy and rebuilt to 16,000 men. Inexperienced divisional and regimental leaders

352 VGD

Rebuilt from Luftwaffe and naval personnel. Poorly trained, lacking experienced officers

▶ *Panthers de-train on a spur line running to Eifel – one of the pieces of the puzzle Allied intelligence officers failed to use wisely. (US National Archives)*

GERMAN ORDER OF BATTLE

GERMAN SIXTH PANZER ARMY, FIRST ASSAULT WAVE

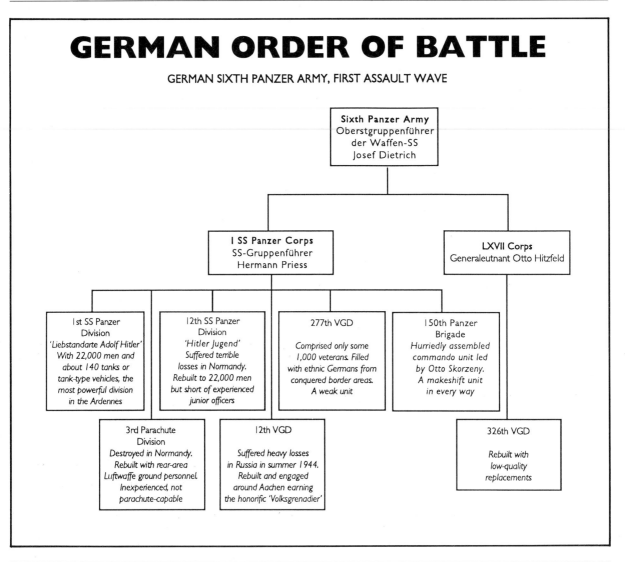

Sixth Panzer Army
Oberstgruppenführer
der Waffen-SS
Josef Dietrich

I SS Panzer Corps
SS-Gruppenführer
Hermann Priess

LXVII Corps
Generaleutnant Otto Hitzfeld

1st SS Panzer Division
'Liebstandarte Adolf Hitler'
With 22,000 men and about 140 tanks or tank-type vehicles, the most powerful division in the Ardennes

12th SS Panzer Division
'Hitler Jugend'
Suffered terrible losses in Normandy. Rebuilt to 22,000 men but short of experienced junior officers

277th VGD
Comprised only some 1,000 veterans. Filled with ethnic Germans from conquered border areas. A weak unit

150th Panzer Brigade
Hurriedly assembled commando unit led by Otto Skorzeny. A makeshift unit in every way

3rd Parachute Division
Destroyed in Normandy. Rebuilt with rear-area Luftwaffe ground personnel. Inexperienced, not parachute-capable

12th VGD
Suffered heavy losses in Russia in summer 1944. Rebuilt and engaged around Aachen earning the honorific 'Volksgrenadier'

326th VGD
Rebuilt with low-quality replacements

▼ *Jagdpanzer IV/70 of SS Panzerjager Abteilung 1.*

mander of VIII Corps charged with holding the Ardennes. During their discussion all realized that the front was thinly held but that it seemed a reasonable risk. No one believed that the hastily trained Volksgrenadier units the Germans used to man the front were capable of offensive action. Furthermore, no one thought a German thrust in the Ardennes could reach an important objective. Only Patton, preparing his own offensive south of the Ardennes, noted in his diary on 24 November: 'The First Army is making a terrible mistake in leaving VIII Corps static, as it is highly probable that the Germans are building up east of them.'

Bradley later claimed that, although he believed a German attack unlikely, he discussed appropriate defensive plans with Middleton: 'If the Germans hit his sector, Middleton was to make a fighting withdrawal – all the way back to the Meuse River if necessary.' The plan relied upon the proven American superiority in mobility whereby reserve armoured divisions would lend assistance from adjacent armies. Planning presumed a limited German spoiling attack of four to six divisions and no one took even this plan too seriously. Had anyone believed an attack possible, the defenders could have fortified. Responding to a post-war question about why this was not done, Middleton said: 'Have you any idea how much manpower and effort would have been required to dig a trench eighty-eight miles long?' While a continuous line was clearly impossible given VIII Corps strength, heavier fortifications at key road intersections and river crossings would have saved many American lives. In the event, the defenders occupied hastily dug foxholes and were without contingency plans for a major German attack.

When von Rundstedt learned of Hitler's plan he was 'staggered' and immediately realized that it was too ambitious for the available resources. He, Model, and von Manteuffel proposed an alternative, which became known as the 'small solution', a pincers attack – one prong of which would strike from the Eifel – with the objective of trapping American forces against the Meuse. Even Dietrich argued against Hitler's plan, but to no avail. Insulated from the incredible hardships and sacrifices German soldiers had made on both the Eastern and Western fronts, Hitler and his en-

tourage lived in a fantasy land. Typical of their unprofessional approach to planning was the question of air support. At one meeting Hitler asked Goering how many aircraft could support the offensive? Goering responded: 'Three thousand.' Hitler turned to von Manteuffel and winked: 'You know Goering. I think we shall have 2,000.' Such laughable planning seriously undermined the chances for the attack.

As ultimately constructed, 'Wacht am Rhein' envisaged a 5.30am assault by three armies striking through the Ardennes from Monschau to Echternach. After crossing the Meuse between Liège and Namur, they would bypass Brussels and capture Antwerp within a week. Cut in two, the western Allies would never recover from the shock, causing their alliance to dissolve and forcing them to sue for a separate peace.

Dietrich's Sixth Panzer Army carried the main effort along the northern flank. Concentrated on a narrow front from Monschau to the Losheim Gap, his first wave comprised four infantry and two élite SS panzer divisions. Curiously, at this stage of the war the Germans had not resolved the doctrinal dispute about whether infantry or armour should attack first. On the Sixth Panzer Army front planners decided that infantry would lead the way to open the sparse road net. The staff expected them to advance three to five miles by noon of the first day. Then the panzers would pass through to begin their race to the Meuse, following the shortest route straight over the Elsenborn Ridge. The powerful 1st SS Panzer Division served as the army's spearhead. Model's plan called for the Meuse crossing on the fourth day.

Von Manteuffel's Fifth Panzer Army, the next army south, had a supporting mission with two major first objectives. Two infantry divisions were to encircle the Schnee Eifel to trap the two forward US 106th Infantry Division regiments. Then the ambitious plan called for them to advance west to capture the key road town of St Vith. Further south, two infantry and three panzer divisions had to secure crossings over the River Our and then race west parallel to Sixth Panzer Army all the way to Antwerp. To begin with, the problem would be bridging the Our. Consequently, here too infantry would lead the way in order to screen engineers who would lay bridges for the panzers heading west. Both panzer armies were to drive relentlessly westward without regard for their flanks.

The weakest of the assault armies, Seventh Army – more a reinforced corps than an army – had a more limited mission somewhat in keeping with its limited mobility and strength. It would conduct a river assault in the Vianden-Echternach area and then march west to protect von Manteuffel's left flank. Planners from Jodl downwards expected the fiercest counterattacks to come from Patton's Third Army, and thus they assigned Seventh Army a largely defensive role. Much hinged upon its ability to advance to key blocking positions along the southern sector.

Hitler hoped to bolster the assault by emulating the winning formula of 1940-1: rapid, deep armoured penetration, paratroop attacks in the rear and infiltration by disguised troops. As an adjunct to the 1st SS Panzer Division's advance, he also laid on Operation 'Greif' (Condor). 'Greif commandos', wearing American uniforms and aided by English-speaking Germans, intended to seize intact at least two Meuse bridges and to spread confusion in the rear by sabotage. In addition, commando extraordinaire Otto Skorzeny commanded a hastily formed, special mechanized brigade of captured or disguised equipment. He was to reinforce the commandos at the Meuse. In the event, however, Operation 'Greif' was to have a very modest impact on the campaign.

Similarly, a proposed parachute drop behind Elsenborn Ridge, Sixth Panzer Army's target, deteriorated from inception to practice when unskilled pilots scattered ill-equipped parachutists all the way from Bonn east of the Rhine to the drop zone. Ten of the 105 Junkers transports delivered the parachutists to the drop area where, once on the ground, they accomplished nothing beyond alarming American rear-echelon soldiers.

Terrain

In the words of the official historian, the Ardennes geography 'leads inevitably to the channelization of large troop movements east to west'. Without excellent traffic control, units would pile up on each other. Once units fixed their direction of attack they faced restricted freedom of manoeuvre since there were few cross-country alternatives. Most roads ran along narrow valley floors. This provided natural blocking points at the valley entrances and exits when the road curved through the slopes. Where the limited roads converged at market towns – Bastogne, St Vith and Manhay, to name a notable three – combat was sure to occur. In addition to the Our and Sauer river lines held by the defenders at the start, the River Ourthe provided a significant mid-point barrier between the start line and the Meuse, while the Rivers Salm and Amblève cut across very rugged terrain perpendicular to Sixth Panzer Army's line of advance. Small-scale tactics, at battalion level and down, confronted severe command and control problems. Rolling, sometimes rugged terrain featured numerous forests and woods. More than is usually the case, combat became a collection of small, independent actions with the combatants and often their leaders having little appreciation of what was really happening. Having passed this way in 1914 and 1940, the Germans understood the terrain restrictions. Terrain obstacles decreased from east to west, so if a rapid breakthrough occurred the panzers could run free. In 1940 reconnaissance elements had reached the Meuse in 24 hours.

For 'Wacht am Rhein', Hitler dictated the strategy, the choice of ground, the allocation of forces and choice of tactics. Traditional Prussian planning and analysis had little role, and thus many German professional officers felt estranged from the concept. Jodl, in planning his first offensive, made a mistake common to inexperienced staff officers: his rigid plans left little room for subordinate initiative and even less to the chance fortunes of war. More than anything, the plan overlooked the difficulty of heavy tanks manoeuvring across wooded ridge lines, along narrow roads and over numerous rivers and streams. These flaws, which meant that the entire counteroffensive was hostage to the possibility that a blown bridge or the determined defence of a road junction could wreck careful timetables, became clear in hindsight. Yet such was the prestige of the German Army, even in 1944, that when the panzers advanced all seemed possible to both attacker and defender.

ASSAULT

Repulse of Sixth Panzer Army

In the pre-dawn light of 16 December, shells and rockets began landing on American positions. The defenders awoke to the greatest American battle of the Second World War. While the Germans attacked all along the 85-mile front, events in three key sectors tell the story of the first 24 hours. Hitler expected Sixth Panzer Army to carry the brunt of the attack. The army's entire scheme of manoeuvre depended upon I SS Panzer Corps achieving a quick breakthrough of the Elsenborn Ridge. The plan called for two Volksgrenadier divisions to crack the American front and then for the SS armour to drive through the gap and on to the Meuse. The odds greatly favoured the Volksgrenadiers. A mere five battalions of the green US 99th Infantry Division covered the sector. But the attackers would need to hurry; sunset was at 4.35.

The key position was the gloomy pine forest in front of the twin villages of Rocherath-Krinkelt, which lay on the forward slopes of the Elsenborn Ridge. Here the initial attack came against K Company, 3rd Battalion, 393rd Infantry. The Germans skilfully followed the opening barrage so that two battalions appeared at Company K's foxhole line before the defenders had a chance to brace themselves for the impact. The attackers quickly overwhelmed all but one platoon. Yet this platoon and the two adjacent companies managed a fighting withdrawal to a line around the battalion command post. Here they held off all comers. Their stout recovery greatly annoyed the com-

▶ *Morale was high among the Germans on the eve of the assault, particularly among the SS such as those shown here. An exuberant SS trooper penned a note to his sister: 'I write during one of the great hours before we attack . . . full of expectation for what the next days will bring . . . we attack and will throw the enemy from our homeland. That is a holy task!' On the back of the envelope he added: 'Ruth! Ruth! Ruth! WE MARCH!' (US National Archives)*

mander of I SS Panzer Corps. In order to force an opening he committed a battalion of SS panzergrenadiers. They managed to surround the 3rd Battalion but, by failing to eliminate the position, could not open the vital road leading west. At steep cost – the defending battalion lost about 300 men – the Americans held.

In an adjacent position, 1st Battalion, 393rd Infantry, confronted the same overwhelming odds. Since its position was more in the open it had excellent fields of fire. The first German assault collapsed in a hurricane of machine-gun, mortar, and artillery fire. Pressured to achieve an im-

mediate breakthrough, the Germans committed another regiment to the assault. But here the attackers' inexperience showed. They assaulted in dense formations with soldiers literally being herded forward by their officers and NCOs. Eventually weight of numbers forced a breach. The last American reserve, 25 men led by a lieutenant from the regimental anti-tank company and 13 men from the headquarters company, counterattacked into the teeth of the German breakthrough. Showing great fighting spirit, this rag-tail group fixed bayonets, charged, killed 28 Germans, and restored the battalion's line. At a

◀ *This rare, scratchy photo shows German self-propelled 150mm artillery in the pre-dawn light of 16 December. (US National Archives)*

◀ *The opening bombardment caught the Americans by surprise and destroyed wire communications, the primary means of tactical communication. Early in the offensive, artillery officers from all three German armies decided to leave behind half the guns and Nebelwerfers because they could not bring ammunition forward. This left subsequent attacks with greatly reduced artillery support. (Wood Collection, US Army Military History Institute)*

The German Assault, to 20 December

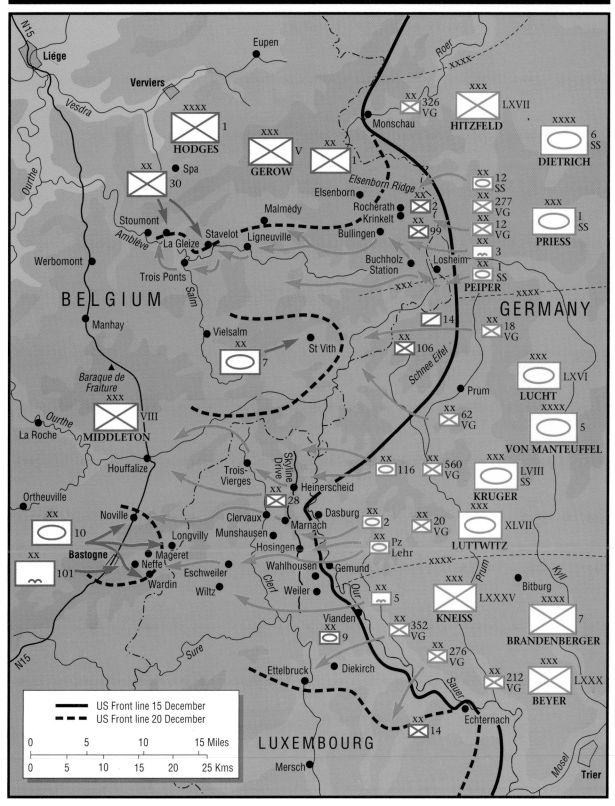

Liège
Eupen
Verviers
Vesdra
Roer
Vesdra
XXXX
Spa
XXXX 1
HODGES
XX 30
Stoumont
Amblève
La Gleize
Stavelot
Ligneuville
Werbomont
Ourthe
Trois Ponts
Salm
BELGIUM
Manhay
Vielsalm
XX 7
St Vith
Baraque de Fraiture
XXX VIII
La Roche
Ourthe
MIDDLETON
Houffalize
Ortheuville
Trois-Vierges
Skyline Drive
Heinerscheid
XX 28
Noville
Clervaux
Marnach
XX 10
Longvilly
Munshausen
Mageret
Hosingen
Bastogne
Neffe
Eschweiler
Wahlhausen
Gemund
XX 101
Wardin
Wiltz
Weiler
Clerf
Our
Sure
Vianden
XX 9
N15
Ettelbruck
Diekirch
LUXEMBOURG
Mersch

XX 326 VG
Monschau
XXX LXVII
HITZFELD
XXXX 6 SS
DIETRICH
XXX V
GEROW
XX 1
Elsenborn Ridge
Elsenborn
Rocherath
Krinkelt
Malmédy
Bullingen
Buchholz Station
Losheim
XX 12 SS
XX 277 VG
XX 2
XX 12 VG
XX 99
XX 3
XX 1 SS
PEIPER
XXX I SS
PRIESS
GERMANY
XXXX
XX 14
XX 18 VG
XX 106
Schnee Eifel
XXX LXVI
LUCHT
Prum
XX 62 VG
XXXX 5
VON MANTEUFFEL
XX 116
XX 560 VG
XXX LVIII SS
KRUGER
XX 2
XX 20 VG
XXX XLVII
LUTTWITZ
Dasburg
XX Pz Lehr
XX 5
XXX LXXXV
KNEISS
Bitburg
XXXX 7
BRANDENBERGER
XX 352 VG
XX 276 VG
XX 212 VG
XXX LXXX
BEYER
Sauer
Mosel
Echternach
XX 14
Trier
Kyll
Prum

US Front line 15 December
US Front line 20 December

0   5   10   15 Miles
0 5 10 15 20 25 Kms

cost of some 400 men the battalion held its position.

During the 38-minute twilight preceding nightfall the Germans began infiltrating gaps in the US position. Strong fighting patrols cut communications. They called out in English hoping to make the defenders reveal themselves. When this failed they sprayed the American position with submachine-gun fire. For any unit it would have been an unnerving experience, yet the green 99th Division stood firm. Hungry, cold, and frightened they awaited the dawn.

Some of the American higher ranking officers did not match the valour of the men they commanded. V Corps' acting commander had anticipated a German counterstroke once his attack on the Roer dams began. The sketchy information he received initially convinced him this was what was taking place. As the day wore on he became more alarmed and set off to visit the 99th Division headquarters. He arrived to find the divisional staff milling about in confusion with everyone shouting at the same time. Leading by example was the divisional commander, playing a piano in the middle of his command post to try to settle his nerves. He insisted that everything was under control.

Forcing the Our

Some 25 miles south, Fifth Panzer Army faced the Americans across the River Our. Army commander von Manteuffel had persuaded Hitler to substitute a short bombardment for the planned two- to three-hour artillery preparation in order to reduce the American alert time. Instead of attacking at 10am, which would leave a mere six daylight hours to gain ground, he proposed to begin before dawn under the illumination of giant searchlights bouncing their light off the clouds. Having spent a night in a front-line pillbox overlooking the American positions, he had learned that the defending 110th Infantry Regiment, 28th Infantry Division (110/28) withdrew its outposts at night. Thus he proposed that his assault troops infiltrate selected areas without any artillery assistance. Hitler agreed with all of this.

At 5.30am, an American lookout in Hosingen on the Skyline Drive (the ridge road running parallel to the Our) called his company commander to report a strange phenomenon: in the distance he saw numerous flickerings of light. Seconds later shells starting bursting all along the Skyline Drive to explain this startling observation.

◀ American artillery fire pinned down many unsupported infantry attacks. Here 155mm artillery fires from position near Wiltz. (US National Archives)

▶ The inability of inexperienced German engineers to span the River Our delayed von Manteuffel's attack. Captured film shows a German supply column crossing a captured American bridge. (US National Archives)

A former Pennsylvania National Guard unit, the 28th Division had earned a good reputation beginning at Normandy; the terrible fighting in the Huertgen Forest, where it lost some 6,100 men, had nearly crippled it. Soldiers had taken to calling its red, bucket-shaped shoulder patch the 'Bloody Bucket'. Sent for rest and refit in the quiet Ardennes sector, the 28th sat squarely in the path of Fifth Panzer Army.

The three regiments comprising the division held a 25-mile front. The left regiment defended good ground and would manage to block the entire LVIII Panzer Corps for a solid 24 hours. The right-hand regiment fought against the under-manned, under-equipped Seventh Army, and it too managed to conduct an organized fighting withdrawal. The centre regiment, 110th Infantry, guarded 15 miles behind the River Our. It faced three German divisions, at odds of more than 10 to 1. Unable to man a continuous defensive line, the regiment occupied company-sized roadblocks on the roads leading up from the Our. Particularly important were the villages of Marnach and Hosingen, through which ran the best roads to Bastogne. Via these roads 19 miles separated the Germans from the critical Bastogne road hub.

The units comprising the assault force included some of the best remaining in the German Army. The veteran 2nd Panzer had 86 tanks, mostly the latest model Panthers, and 20 assault guns. The 26th VGD counted some 17,000 men in its ranks. Unlike other Volksgrenadier units, it had won its honorific title in battle and was one of the few to be rebuilt in the old organization of three infantry battalions per regiment. Both divisions had been brought up to strength with superior replacements, yet both shared the army-wide lack of mechanized transport. In contrast, the experienced Panzer Lehr Division, the corps' third assault division, had been sucked into the defensive fighting against Patton's Third Army in November. It had not recovered from its heavy losses and numbered a mere 57 Mark IV and Panther tanks. Most important, such was the German material poverty at this stage of the war that although Fifth Panzer Army held a formidable qualitative and quantitative edge in equipment, it lacked good bridging equipment for spanning the Our. Until its engineers manhandled pontoons down narrow, slippery roads and fastened them into place, the infantry of 26th VGD would have to carry the fight alone without supporting heavy weapons or tanks.

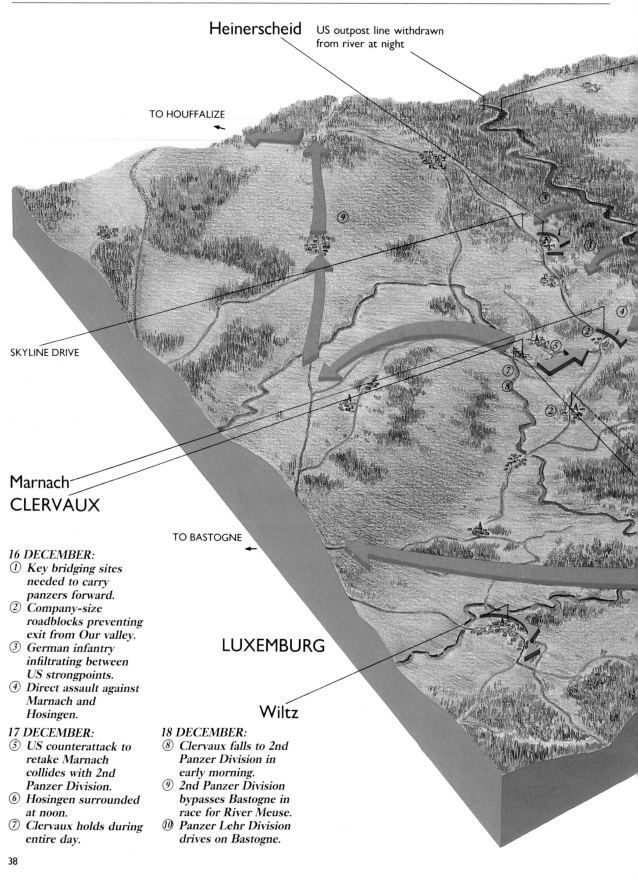

Heinerscheid

US outpost line withdrawn
from river at night

TO HOUFFALIZE

SKYLINE DRIVE

Marnach
CLERVAUX

TO BASTOGNE

LUXEMBURG

Wiltz

16 DECEMBER:
① *Key bridging sites needed to carry panzers forward.*
② *Company-size roadblocks preventing exit from Our valley.*
③ *German infantry infiltrating between US strongpoints.*
④ *Direct assault against Marnach and Hosingen.*

17 DECEMBER:
⑤ *US counterattack to retake Marnach collides with 2nd Panzer Division.*
⑥ *Hosingen surrounded at noon.*
⑦ *Clervaux holds during entire day.*

18 DECEMBER:
⑧ *Clervaux falls to 2nd Panzer Division in early morning.*
⑨ *2nd Panzer Division bypasses Bastogne in race for River Meuse.*
⑩ *Panzer Lehr Division drives on Bastogne.*

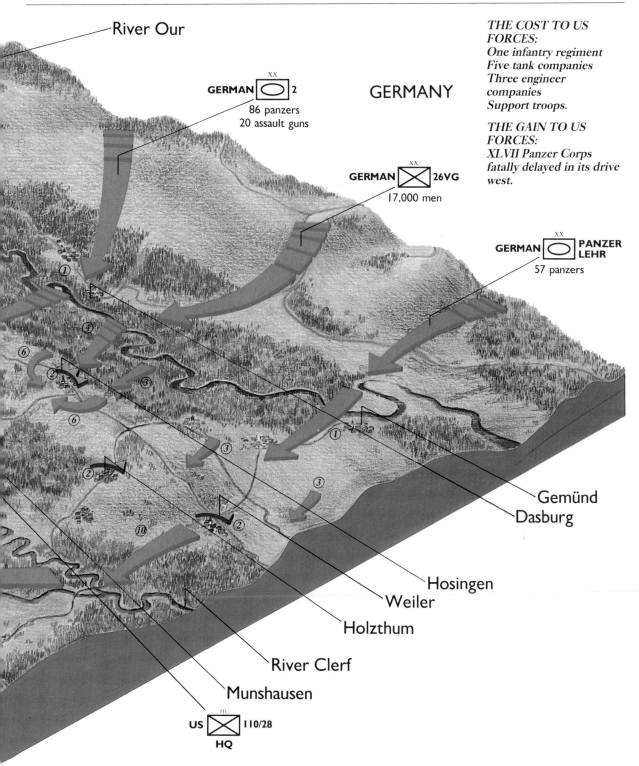

River Our

GERMAN [⬭] 2
86 panzers
20 assault guns

GERMANY

GERMAN [⊠] 26VG
17,000 men

THE COST TO US
FORCES:
One infantry regiment
Five tank companies
Three engineer
companies
Support troops.

THE GAIN TO US
FORCES:
XLVII Panzer Corps
fatally delayed in its drive
west.

GERMAN [⬭] PANZER
LEHR
57 panzers

Gemünd
Dasburg

Hosingen

Weiler

Holzthum

River Clerf

Munshausen

US [⊠] 110/28
HQ

US 110/28TH DIVISION'S DELAYING ACTIONS

16 to 18 December 1944.

Some of the shells and rockets from XLVII Panzer Corps' 554 artillery pieces and Nebelwerfers landed amid the 110th's headquarters at Clervaux and awakened the regimental commander, Colonel Hurley Fuller. Turning to his assistant Fuller asked: 'What do you make of it?' The officer replied: 'All this big stuff is a sure sign we're in for a fight.'

To ensure rapid progress, von Manteuffel had directed his men to emulate First World War infiltration tactics ('Hutier tactics') and bypass most pockets of resistance. However, since Marnach and Hosingen blocked the two major westward roads, von Manteuffel demanded that they should be seized quickly by a direct assault.

▲ Once armoured support, such as this assault gun, crossed the Our, they spearheaded the attack against the 110/28. Lacking effective anti-tank support, the American defence collapsed. (US National Archives)

◀ The dispersal of American tanks into 'penny packets' led to futile armoured counterattacks. This Sherman turret shows the all too common result. In 10 minutes, an American light tank company attempting to counterattack to support the 110/28th lost eight tanks to concealed German high-velocity guns and three to panzerfausts. (US National Archives)

Surprise, coupled with dense fog, allowed the German assault companies to advance to almost on top of the American positions before detection. In some cases the attackers annihilated entire platoons before they could react. Yet many defenders responded with veteran aplomb. Surprised at their guns, Battery C, 109th Field Artillery Battalion, lowered their muzzles to deliver point-blank shells in the attackers' faces. Outside Consthum, an anti-aircraft gunner spotted the attackers, waved them forward in friendly fashion, fingered the button of his quad-50 machine-guns and knocked down nearly 100 Germans in a matter of seconds.

In many places American mortar and artillery fire pinned assault columns to the ground for the balance of the day. In others, such as at Hosingen where the first wave overran a platoon south of the village, the Germans failed to press their advantage. This key village held all day. Nearby, after blundering through a minefield, the panzer-grenadiers of the 2nd Panzer Division assaulted Marnach. Thoroughly alerted, B Company shot the attack apart. But as the day progressed, many surviving defenders began to realize that significant numbers of Germans were bypassing their positions and marching west.

Unlike most higher ranking officers, the regimental commander quickly realized that a major attack was under way. Fighting short-handed from the beginning, with one of his three infantry battalions providing the divisional reserve, Fuller requested reinforcements as soon as the communication line was restored at about 9am. The divisional commander, Major General Norman Cota, refused to commit his only infantry reserve so early in the battle. Instead he sent two tank companies, 34 Shermans. Confronting break-throughs all along his front, Fuller split the tanks into the type of 'penny packets' that so attracted the scorn of experienced German panzer leaders. While this perhaps necessary tactic bolstered many of the beleaguered defenders, the tanks failed to exert a decisive influence. Worse, in the marching and counter-marching no one realized that the two platoons that had been ordered to Marnach did not stay there.

The German infantry suffered heavily in their unsupported attacks against the 110/28th. By afternoon German engineers had finally completed the critical bridges at Dasburg and Gemund. German armour slowly debouched up the narrow, muddy roads of the Our valley towards Skyline Drive. One by one American positions began to face new infantry assaults backed by armour. A platoon at Wahlhausen called in artillery on its own position to try to stop the German armour. The tactic failed and only one American escaped.

Desperate, Fuller organized and armed rear-echelon personnel and established roadblocks to try to halt the attack. Cooks, clerks, and MPs were given a carbine or a bazooka and told to hold at all costs. Middleton, the corps commander, had abandoned his pre-battle plan to conduct a fighting withdrawal in the event of a German attack. Instead he ordered everyone to defend in place until their positions were 'completely untenable'.

In spite of the overwhelming odds and the confused commitment of reserves, by the end of 16 December the 110th Regiment had lost only three defended positions. Partially the success came from the unsuccessful 'Hutier tactics': time and again, while trying to pass between the American outposts, the Germans found themselves raked in flank by vigilant defenders. And partially success resulted from the slow German bridge-laying together with the poor roads that kept the supporting armour from joining battle. Mostly, however, success stemmed from the intrepid fighting of the isolated infantry, handfuls of veterans stiffening numerous green replacements and jointly refusing to yield. Already the Germans were falling seriously behind schedule.

Through the Losheim Gap

At only one point did the Germans achieve the type of clean breakthrough that 'Wacht am Rhein' required. The seven-mile-wide Losheim Gap provided an east to west invasion route that the Germans had used in 1870, 1914, and 1940. Remarkably, it was the sector on the Ardennes front most lightly held by the Americans. One-half of the 14th Cavalry Group, about 900 men, was responsible for the southern five miles. Nominally, they were attached to the adjacent 106th Infantry

◀ *In mud and snow, towed anti-tank guns such as this 3in model, photographed by the Germans on 17 December, could not be moved fast enough. Direct fire or infantry assault made the task of limbering the gun difficult and often knocked out the tow vehicle. (US National Archives)*

Division. But the 106th had only entered the line four days previously, and its commander had yet to meet the 14th Cavalry commander. Moreover, the inter-corps boundary between V and VIII Corps was in the middle of the gap, and thus: 'Though two soldiers can shake hands across this boundary, the chain of command separates them by a hundred miles.' Assigned a static position, the lightly armed cavalry sacrificed their one strength, mobility. Beyond the 14th's sector, no soldiers occupied the two northern miles of the gap. Here hourly jeep patrols provided the only security.

The boundary between Sixth and Fifth Panzer Armies also ran through the southern portion of the gap. OKW drew this boundary to provide a swift route west for the 1st SS Panzer Division, giving von Manteuffel's men only enough room to slice around the northern end of the Schnee Eifel to encircle the two American regiments stationed on the high ground. As elsewhere, German infantry had to open the route for the panzers. Accordingly, following the opening bombardment came the 3rd Parachute Division against the northern portion of the 14th Cavalry.

Elements of the 3rd Parachute Division reinforced with tanks faced two cavalry platoons, two reconnaissance platoons, a TD company and headquarters units. In effect, the attackers confronted small islands of defence featuring two to four towed anti-tank guns with a handful of riflemen and machine-gunners. The defenders recovered quickly from their surprise and German inexperience showed itself as the 3rd Parachute's attack dissolved into a series of stumbling, uncoordinated lurches forward. But slowly numbers told. The regular jeep patrol crossing the two-mile-wide void north of the 14th Cavalry reported the area 'crawling with Krauts!' Further south, two regiments of von Manteuffel's 18th VGD backed by 40 75mm assault guns and numerous self-propelled tank destroyers attacked Troop A (a company-sized formation) and one platoon of Troop C, 18th Cavalry Squadron. The attackers suffered heavy losses, trading casualties for speed, but inexorably they overpowered the defenders.

Most defenders fought well, but there were exceptions. At one small village a last radio message reported enemy assault guns 'seventy-five yards from CP, firing direct fire. Out.' After losing three killed, the remaining 87-man garrison surrendered. Reserve cavalry elements failed to stabilize the situation, their intervention weakened by their colonel's cowardice. He fled to the rear 'in search of extra ammunition'. By noon the Germans had either captured, surrounded, or were about to assault every village in the Losheim Gap. And by nightfall the situation had badly deteriorated, with the 14th Cavalry scattered and out of touch with headquarters. However well they had fought during the day, at night the 14th's dispersed elements grew nervous, shuffled positions, and were thrown off balance. Long columns of vehicles with rear-area soldiers clinging to their decks began to hasten to the rear. The situation verged on panic. The appearance of Tiger tanks at dawn on 17 December produced an accordion-like series of retreats and gave the attackers their breakthrough. The cavalry's failure to hold placed the GIs on the Schnee Eifel in great peril.

While one German pincer moved through the Losheim Gap the other advanced south of the Schnee Eifel. The threatened link-up would surround the two regiments defending the high ground. The defenders did not comprehend the true situation. Secure in good positions, they spent an easy day repulsing an occasional German patrol. Proud of their ability to hold their ground in this, their first combat, they did not realize that they confronted an exceptionally thin screen from a German replacement battalion and that the real decision was taking place deep on either flank.

In St Vith the divisional commander, Major General Alan Jones, looked at his situation map and saw the danger. Around noon he telephoned his corps commander to ask permission to withdraw the units atop the Schnee Eifel. Middleton demurred (later saying that he had worried that if the two green regiments started to the rear they 'might go half-way to Paris') and Jones, anxious not to appear jumpy with his first command, did not press the case.

▼ *A US M4A3E8 heavily protected by sandbags.*

By nightfall the situation had worsened, so Jones called again. The generals spoke on an unsecured, improvised telephone line. Fearful of German eavesdropping, they talked using stilted riddles and code words. Consequently, when Middleton hung up he told his staff that he had told Jones: 'to pull his regiments off the Schnee Eifel'. At the other end Jones reported to his staff that Middleton required the division to hold in place. Some of the 106th's officers realized the implications of the decision to remain in position. Jones' G-2 wrote that evening: 'The enemy is capable of pinching off the Schnee Eifel area. . . at any time.' The stage was set for the largest American surrender in the Second World War.

Reactions at the Top

Spread thinly on the ground, with communications knocked out by the initial German bombardment, the front-line defenders had little knowledge of anything beyond their immediate sector. Their reports seeping up the chain of command gave a fragmentary picture of the situation at the end of 16 December. Some reports from divisional com-

manders did not help. As late as 4.15pm, 28th Division reported that 'the situation for the division is well in hand'. By nightfall, proud of his inexperienced unit's conduct during the day, the commander of the 99th Division told V Corps 'that the situation was in hand and all quiet'.

As early as 7am the First Army commander, Lieutenant General Courtney Hodges, learned of German attacks. He placed a regimental combat team on alert. At 10.30am he ordered that CCA/9th Armored Division be released from the Roer dams attack and sent to support Middleton. After these commendable initial reactions, a curious torpor overcame Hodges. He believed he faced a German spoiling attack and was reluctant to cancel the Roer drive. He clung to this view into the night even after both V and VIII Corps headquarters had in hand captured German orders announcing that a great counteroffensive was under way. Hodges' V Corps commander wavered between concern over events on his right flank – his lone supply route and potential avenue of withdrawal was through the twin villages of Rocherath-Krinkelt – and a desire to press the Roer attack. VIII Corps commander, Middleton, was in no such quandary. He realized that the German effort was much more than a spoiling attack and that he faced impending crisis. Accordingly, early in the day he had issued Hitler-like orders to all units, with the exception, he thought, of the 106th Division, to stand firm and defend in place. To a certain extent the American higher command was working at cross purposes. The surprise assault had confused them.

Buffered from events at the front, the day saw the army group commander in transit to SHAEF at Versailles. Bradley arrived to press his case to Eisenhower for additional infantry replacements. An officer interrupted the meeting with news from Middleton. First reports indicated German attacks at five points. Most American officers, including Bradley, thought here was the anticipated spoiling attack launched in response to the First Army drive on the Roer dams and Patton's impending offensive. They did not want to play into German hands by diverting troops from those offensives. As the evening wore on, additional reports informed SHAEF that eight divisions previously not identified on the Ardennes front were attacking Middleton. A staff officer commented to the now thoroughly alarmed Bradley: 'Well, Brad, you've been wishing for a counterattack. Now it looks as though you've got it.' Bradley replied: 'A counterattack, yes. But I'll be damned if I wanted one this big.'

Upon first news of the attack, Eisenhower alone sensed it was something big. Although there were only four uncommitted American divisions on the entire Western front, the Supreme Commander recommended Bradley send two armoured divisions, the 7th from the north and the 10th from the south, to help Middleton. Bradley agreed. This quick response proved one of the campaign's key decisions. Still the situation did not appear overly grave. Bradley and Eisenhower spent the evening celebrating Ike's recent promotion by playing five rubbers of bridge over a bottle of champagne.

Across the lines at German army level, the most confident general was the commander of Seventh Army. He had expected little from his weak army, yet as he surveyed the map pins marking his progress he felt he was on the verge of a breakthrough. His forces had managed to cross the River Sauer and establish several lodgements within the American position and had forced the defending 4th Infantry Division to request reinforcements from the embattled Middleton. In contrast, the first day's progress disappointed von Manteuffel. He hoped that by continuing the attack during the night he could return to his ambitious schedule. At the neighbouring Sixth Panzer Army, Sepp Dietrich's chief of staff, who did most of the strategic thinking for his commanding officer, worried that failure to break through would allow American reinforcements to flow rapidly south. He ordered the ill-prepared German parachutists to jump that night to block this flow. Here was wishful thinking in the extreme. It was left to the old veteran von Rundstedt to describe the true situation. He briefed Hitler that while the attack had achieved total surprise, Sixth Panzer Army had failed to achieve a breakthrough and this jeopardized the army's chances of reaching the Meuse.

Hitler typically did not listen to pessimistic news. Believing his troops were on the verge of a breakthrough, delighted that the weather was supposed to remain bad and thus ground Allied aircraft, he exalted: 'Everything has changed in the West! Success – complete success – is now in our grasp.'

But by the end of the first day the Germans had failed to achieve the expected breakthrough. Even green American units had stood firm in the face of surprise while slowing the German advance and inflicting irreplaceable losses. Contrary to Hitler's cherished belief, the Allied High Command, in the person of Eisenhower, was responding in a coordinated manner by immediately drawing upon armoured reserves from two adjacent armies. However, tomorrow would tell all. The first day's attacks had disclosed weaknesses in the American position. Bridges had been seized or built, the panzers stood poised to roll.

▲Men of 1st SS
Panzergrenadier
Regiment.

BREAKTHROUGH

Collapse in the Centre

While the American generals worked, according to their varying capacities, to comprehend the German offensive, along the Fifth Panzer Army front von Manteuffel sought to get back on schedule by continuing the attack through the night. Infiltration tactics worked much better in the dark. Assault groups penetrated between American positions and began picking off the artillery positions supporting the front-line village garrisons. They overran some artillery and forced others to displace hurriedly to the rear.

By dawn, tanks of the 2nd Panzer Division were moving forward to attack the Clerf river crossings at Clervaux. Simultaneously, Fuller committed his reserves to retake Marnach. It was an amazing spectacle: a couple of infantry companies and one company of light tanks versus substantial elements of an entire panzer corps. Without artillery support, the American infantry could make no headway. Eighteen light tanks advancing from Heinerscheid ran into concealed German assault guns and lost eight vehicles. Panzerfausts knocked out three more as the effort collapsed. Remarkably, a

▼ *Although front-line defenders quickly captured copies of the German attack order, not until the morning of 17 December did Bradley and Eisenhower learn of these orders. The morning's Ultra decodes provided von Rundstedt's attack order: 'The hour of destiny has struck. Mighty offensive armies face the Allies. Everything is at stake. More than mortal deeds are required as a holy duty to the Fatherland.' Here a posed German photograph taken in the Ardennes on 17 December shows assaulting infantry. (US National Archives)*

third attack featuring a platoon of Shermans carrying an infantry platoon moved from Munshausen and reconquered part of Marnach. But they could not hold alone against counterattacking tanks and panzergrenadiers, so Fuller ordered them to retreat.

At 10.30am a tank company from CCR/9 Armored Division unexpectedly reinforced Fuller in Clervaux. The aggressive colonel split the 17 Shermans into three platoons and used them to reinforce his crumbling positions. Entering combat for the first time, the tanks ran straight into the growing might of the 2nd Panzer Division and were nearly annihilated.

Spearheaded by assault guns and tanks that had finally extricated themselves from the Our valley, Fifth Panzer Army began to overwhelm the 110/28. By noon on the 17th the Germans had surrounded the key roadblock at Hosingen. Frustrated at his lack of progress, the commander of XLVII Panzer Corps committed the Panzer Lehr's advanced guard to the fray. The defenders' five remaining tanks moved to counter one attack after another, but by the evening the Germans had forced K Company into a small perimeter around company headquarters and the regimental engineers into another small pocket across the village. After an epic defence, the Hosingen defenders finally surrendered.

Also during the 17th the attackers brought increasing weight to bear directly against regimental headquarters in Clervaux. Fuller's remaining platoon of Shermans duelled with the German Mark IVs on the heights and managed to block the road by destroying one tank. But by now the attackers had multiple routes to enter the town and Fuller's situation became desperate. He requested permission to withdraw; but Middleton's 'hold at all costs' order remained in effect. The final stand came in an old castle that dominated the town. From its crenellated walls American snipers picked off unwary Germans in the streets below. However, after exhausting their supply of bazooka ammunition, they were helpless to prevent the flood of German armour moving west. At noon on the 18th, a German tank battered down the wooden doors of the castle and forced the surviving defenders to surrender.

The fall of Clervaux and the parallel collapse of the remainder of the 28th Division's positions ended the unit's delaying actions before Bastogne. At a time in the war when American units did not expect to suffer heavy losses, the 110th Infantry Regiment along with the men and vehicles of five tank companies, the equivalent of three combat engineer companies, and supporting tank destroyers, artillery and service troops had all been virtually destroyed. In the words of the official historian: 'without the gallant bargain struck by the 110th Infantry and its allied units – men for time – the German plans for a coup-de-main at Bastogne would have turned to accomplished fact.'

The pressure was now transferred to other American troops who had to determine whether the hours and minutes won by the tremendous fighting spirit displayed by the 28th Division would be sufficient to preserve Bastogne from the advancing German tanks.

The Defence of the Twin Villages

Unlike Fifth Panzer Army, Sixth Panzer Army did not press its attack during the night. When it resumed its attacks at dawn, for the second day the combat around the twin villages of Rocherath-Krinkelt was of the utmost importance. It was a position the Americans had to hold. It had the only usable escape route for the 2nd and 99th Divisions. Attacked frontally by three divisions of I SS Corps, flanked by the breakthrough in the Losheim Gap, Major General Walter Robertson first had to extract his units concentrated in the north-east for the Roer dams offensive. Fortunately, the day before he had disobeyed Hodges' order to continue the 2nd Division's attack against the dams. Furthermore, Robertson had made the key decision to send two battalions to reinforce the defenders in front of the twin villages.

Stiffened by the 2nd Division veterans, the 99th Division managed to hold its position. Behind its protective screen vast vehicular columns clogged the road westwards. Once the 2nd Division arrived to provide a backstop, the 99th Division had to disengage and withdraw. This exceedingly difficult feat of disengaging through the twin villages bottleneck while under attack is described by an

American company commander: 'Wave after wave of fanatically screaming German infantry stormed the slight tree-covered rise held by the three platoons. A continuous hail of fire exuded from their weapons, answered by volley after volley from the defenders. Germans fell right and left. The few rounds of artillery we did succeed in bringing down caught the attackers in the draw to our front, and we could hear their screams of pain when the small-arms fire would slacken. But still they came!'

When five Tiger tanks joined the assault, the company's two supporting Shermans 'bugged out' – in vain an American officer tried to convince the Shermans to stand, but the tank crews replied that it would be suicide to face the Tigers. Meanwhile, the German tanks began methodically to pound

▶ *One of the units blocked by the stubborn American defence of the twin villages was Skorzeny's 150th Panzer Brigade. False side-panels along with American insignia disguise this 150th Tiger as an American M-10 TD. The Royal Tiger gave its 5-man crew a crushing superiority in tank v. tank duels. At 68 tonnes, the heaviest tank of the war, it carried turret armour more than 7 inches thick. Driven by a 700-horsepower engine it had a top speed of 26 miles per hour. More important, its extra-wide tracks and superior drive system, which allowed it to turn quickly by reversing one track's direction while the opposite one continued pulling, gave it superb tactical agility. Its 88mm long-barrelled, high-velocity gun fired a 22-pound shell easily capable of penetrating the front of a Sherman tank. (US National Archives)*

▶ *One of the war's famous photographs, captured from the Germans, showing one of Peiper's amphibious cars during the advance. The faint lines on the signs are from the pen of the American censor who obscured the place names on the originals before releasing them. (US National Archives)*

the American foxhole line at 75 yards' range. With their few bazookas knocked out or out of ammunition, the defenders had no counter. Slowly at first, and then with some panic the company broke.

Fortuitously, the Sixth Panzer Army commander was unhappy with his rate of progress and chose this moment to order the 12th SS Panzer Division to redeploy through the Losheim Gap. His decision eased the pressure on the hard-pressed defenders. The Americans milled in disorder at the twin villages front on the night of 17 December, but the Germans did not break through. On the 19th the 2nd Division pulled back to the Elsenborn Ridge position. Here the two divisions joined the 1st Division to form a formidable defence backed by bountiful artillery. The crushing defensive artillery kept the Germans at bay for the remainder of the campaign. On Hitler's

◄ *On both sides a prisoner's fate often depended upon the mood of his captors. If enraged, having just seen their buddies killed, or if it were deemed inconvenient to escort prisoners to the rear, they shot them. Patton noted in his diary on 4 January: 'There were also some unfortunate incidents in the shooting of prisoners (I hope we can conceal this).' However, only the Germans executed prisoners as a matter of policy. Here lie American victims of the infamous Malmédy massacre. (US National Archives)*

◄ *The puny 57mm gun provided the main anti-tank weapon the Americans deployed against Peiper. Some 250 Tigers, including 45 Royal Tigers, participated in the offensive. The only realistic American tactic was to attack the tank's rear. However, the mud and snow limited off-road mobility, thus reducing many tank encounters to frontal slugging matches. Here the inferior American weapons and armaments had no chance. Aware of their inferiority, all too often US tankers 'bugged out' leaving the hapless GI to fend for himself. (US National Archives)*

▼ *Panzerkampfwagen IV Ausf J of the 1st SS Panzer Regiment.*

orders, the Germans continued futile attacks here until 24 December.

Robertson's battlefield leadership coupled with the 99th Division's valour allowed the formation of a barrier on the northern shoulder squarely blocking Sixth Panzer Army's intended drive west. As described by Sandhurst historian John Pimlott: 'It was a major contribution to eventual American victory.'

Peiper

From the beginning, some of the keener German officers appreciated the importance of the delayed breakthrough. One in particular was deeply disturbed. Obersturmbannführer Joachim Peiper expected to be driving through the break in American lines in the early morning of the 16th. Instead, he had spent the day in a fuel-consuming traffic jam as his regiment waited for the leading 3rd Parachute Division to clear the way. At last he ordered his tankers to plough through the clogged roads and arrived around midnight in the Losheim

Gap to visit the spearheading paratroopers. He found them resting, awaiting the dawn before advancing, worried about mined roads. Peiper asked if the colonel had personally scouted the route of advance. 'No,' came the reply. Peiper told the colonel to put one of his battalions on the back of the SS tanks. Henceforth his SS men would make their own breakthrough.

At dawn in the Losheim Gap, a scouting American armoured car watched American vehicles with blackout lights stream to the rear. Suddenly appeared a walking soldier carrying a white handkerchief to guide the 'biggest damn tank' the car commander had ever seen. It was Peiper's command.

Peiper had earned a ruthless reputation for leading his tank unit on the Eastern Front. Known as the 'Blowtorch Battalion' after the destruction of two Russian villages and their inhabitants, having once claimed 2,000 enemy killed and only three captured, Peiper now brought his unit west to spearhead the drive to the Meuse. His division, the 1st SS Panzer, was undiluted by large numbers of poorly trained Luftwaffe or Navy replacements, and was the strongest in Sixth Panzer Army. Yet the lack of roads prevented its commitment as a division. Accordingly, the divisional commander divided his unit into four marching groups. Peiper's powerful Kampfgruppe (battlegroup) comprised 100 Mark IVs and Panthers, along with a fully motorized panzergrenadier unit. During their advance they would be joined by Royal Tigers belonging to the 501st SS Panzer Detachment. Peiper, as the armoured spearhead, had strict instructions to follow a prescribed route west and to keep moving without regard to his flanks. He would both spearhead the breakthrough while creating chaos in the American rear. The German high command believed such chaos, augmented by terror tactics, would cause a quick collapse among the 'soft' Americans.

From Buchholz Station, near where the American armoured car spotted him, Peiper trailed behind an American column as it retreated westward. His high fuel consumption in the previous day's traffic jams forced Peiper to divert north to capture a fuel dump at Bullingen. At this point Peiper faced a choice. He could continue west to the Meuse or turn to cut off the 2nd and 99th Infantry Divisions on the Elsenborn Ridge. These divisions had only a single, narrow, muddy farm track by which to retreat. No defenders stood between Peiper and this escape route – conceivably he could cut off some 30,000 men. The 99th's commander realized the situation: Peiper 'had the key to success within his hands but did not know it'.

Restocked, the SS colonel split his column and turned west. The panzergrenadiers under his subordinate proceeded to commit the most infamous atrocity of the war in western Europe. Mindful of their mission to sow terror, they shot some 85 prisoners just south of Malmédy. Kampfgruppe Peiper had already shot prisoners in Bullingen and were to kill more along with Belgian civilians in the ensuing days. But it was the discovery of these bodies strewn in a field that taught the defenders what kind of soldiers they faced. Word spread quickly about the massacre and considerably stiffened American resolve in the

▼ *Between 16 and 22 December, engineers formed the backbone of the US rear-area defence. Their activities delayed the spearheading panzers time and again. According to the official historian, 'a squad equipped with sufficient TNT could, in the right spot, do more to slow the enemy advance than a company armed with rifles and machine guns'. Peiper put it more succinctly. Gazing at the engineers' work, such as this blown bridge at Stavelot, he muttered: 'Those damned engineers.' (US Army Military History Institute)*

days ahead. The Malmédy massacre had the opposite effect Hitler had anticipated.

Peiper's column was now operating in the American rear. Some combat engineers, hastily collected by their colonel, were all that blocked his route west. Shortly after 4pm the colonel reported to First Army at Spa that a strong German column was as far west as Malmédy. The news shocked Hodges' headquarters. Up to this point, Hodges had believed the gravest threats were at St Vith and Bastogne. If the Germans captured Malmédy they could strike north against army headquarters and across First Army's line of communications or north-west towards Liège, the biggest Allied supply dump on the continent. For the first time, Hodges appreciated the dimensions of the German effort. He ordered the 30th Infantry Division to head for Malmédy, but they could not arrive until the following morning. He scraped together the only troops he could find including his headquarters security detachments and sent them to block Peiper. In the meantime, everything depended upon the ability of a series of combat engineer roadblocks to delay Peiper.

About 5pm Peiper departed Ligneuville to seize the bridge at Stavelot. The execrable roads – Peiper later complained that the route was suitable 'not for tanks but for bicycles' - - restricted his advance to a narrow path along a cliff. In the dark, thirteen combat engineers armed with a few mines, a .30-cal. machine-gun, and a bazooka confronted Peiper's advance guard. They belonged to the 291st Engineer Combat Battalion and until a few hours ago had expected to perform their routine work at a local saw-mill. Then came the electrifying order to head for Stavelot and establish a roadblock against a possible German advance. As they worked, Private Bernard Goldstein stood guard by the road. He heard engine noises and tightened his grasp on his M1 rifle. As the vehicles approached, Goldstein made out German voices: they were the paratroopers Peiper had commandeered to ride aboard his tanks. The private shouted: 'Halt!' The return fire sent him scurrying over the hill, but he had alerted his comrades that the Germans were here. Two engineers went forward to investigate, snapped off a few rifle shots, and retired. The bazooka team fired, although they had no target. And then it was over. The tanks retired while the engineers hurried off in the opposite direction to Stavelot.

After a rapid advance deep into First Army's rear, Peiper's column had met the weakest of opposition and inexplicably coiled up for the night. Peiper himself was probably not with the leading tanks when they halted. He accepted his subordinate's appraisal that the Americans held the hill in strength. His own fatigue undoubtedly clouded his judgment. His column was strung out over 25 miles of poor, sodden roads and his men were tired. These factors partially explain Peiper's decision to halt. The delay, by the narrowest, enabled Hodges to bring the 30th Division from the north to block Peiper's penetration.

Peiper resumed his advance at 8am on the 18th. He rushed the Stavelot bridge – the demolition wires apparently sabotaged by a Greif commando unit – and headed for the next river crossing at Trois Ponts. Again combat engineers intervened, this time by blowing two bridges and forcing Peiper from his direct route. Losing precious time and consuming irreplaceable fuel, Peiper turned north towards La Gleize. He captured an intact bridge but his success was short-lived. A rare weather break brought US fighter-bombers and forced his command to take cover. Simultaneously elements of the 30th Division blocked further westward movement. Peiper withdrew at nightfall on the 18th into La Gleize and Stoumont. Operating in near total isolation, his rearward radio link failed during the day, Peiper experienced enough reverses on 18 December to sense stiffening opposition. He did not know that the ring around his unit was tightening.

Early on the 19th a battalion of the 30th Division recaptured Stavelot, thus isolating Peiper from the balance of the 1st SS Division. Over the next three days the Germans tried desperately to carve a supply route to Peiper's isolated spearhead. They failed. Meanwhile, employing overwhelming force, the American vice around Peiper squeezed. On 23 December Peiper abandoned his mission and led a remnant of his unit on foot back to German lines. Kampfgruppe Peiper, the unit that had come closest to fulfilling Hitler's scheme, had failed.

▼SdKfz 251/3 Ausf D of the 2nd SS Panzergrenadier Regiment.

▼Panzerkampfwagen V Panther Ausf G of 1st SS Panzer Regiment.

RACE TO BASTOGNE

To the Outskirts

The market town of Bastogne was the hub for seven major roads. When the 1940 blitzkrieg had exploded through the Ardennes, Bastogne had been one of the first German objectives. In 1944, OKW planners well recognized Bastogne's importance. Believing that its early occupation was critical, they managed to persuade Hitler to modify his plan in order to seize the town. Then OKW's operational inexperience showed: planners failed to assign a force commensurate with the objective's importance. Unless it found Bastogne lightly defended, XLVII Panzer Corps intended to bypass Bastogne and head west. The 26th VGD received the mission of capturing Bastogne by the third day. This was much to ask, even of a unit as good as 'the Old 26th', since the division first had to seize river crossings at the Our and Clerf to open the way for the panzers and then march unsupported to Bastogne.

From the American perspective Bastogne seemed terribly vulnerable. Thirty-six hours after the offensive began, Hodges had seen VIII Corps' centre give way. He had thrown all available reinforcements into the battle, so now he was compelled to request help from the SHAEF reserve. On the morning of 18 December, Eisenhower's last reserves, the 101st and 82nd Airborne Divisions, began racing to block the German breakthrough. But it would take time for them to arrive, and it was not at all clear whether the Germans would grant the time.

The delaying action in front of Bastogne had begun the previous evening. Ten minutes after word reached VIII Corps headquarters that the Germans had crossed the Clerf, Middleton ordered his sole armoured reserve, CCR/9th

▶ *Confusion continued in the American high command on 17 December. However, Patton comprehended the situation and entered in his diary that day: 'The German attack is on a wide front and moving fast . . . This may be a feint . . . although at the moment it looks like the real thing.' This posed propaganda photograph shows German troops passing a knocked out American armoured car. (US National Archives)*

Armored Division, to move 'without delay', establish two roadblocks on the main paved road to Bastogne, and hold 'at all costs'. By midnight, 17 December, CCR/9 was in position between Clervaux and Bastogne. By mid-morning of 18 December, panzers had appeared to probe Task Force Rose's roadblock, which comprised 17 Shermans, a company of armoured infantry and an engineer platoon. The inexperienced American infantry broke under German tank fire and headed for the rear.

By 2pm, Middleton had learned that: 'TF Rose . . . is as good as surrounded. . . have counted 16 German tanks. . . TF is being hit from 3 sides . . . Recommend that they fight their way out. They could use 2 platoons of A/52d Armd Inf Bn [the last CCR infantry reserve], everything else is committed.' It is indicative of the paucity of American strength that a hard-pressed captain who faced a charging panzer division had to radio corps headquarters to secure release of reserves and that the only reserves available were two armoured infantry platoons. Middleton, desperate to buy time for reinforcements to arrive at Bastogne, refused Task Force Rose's request to retreat. A handful of Americans broke free at dusk only to stumble into an ambush further west. Only a few vehicles and crews reached Bastogne.

The other, larger roadblock suffered an even more dismal fate. At dusk Mark IVs and Panthers attacked. Equipped with new infra-red night-sight devices, the Panthers picked off the outclassed Shermans. When the roadblock commander was killed, the defence collapsed. At this point, on the evening of 18 December, no formed troops stood between the 2nd Panzer Division and Bastogne. However, according to plan, this division's business lay further west. At a road junction near Longvilly, Colonel Lauchert turned his unit north to bypass Bastogne and headed for the Meuse.

The 2nd Panzer Division's running mate, the Panzer Lehr Division, also had an excellent chance to capture the crucial crossroads. Major General Fritz Bayerlein had finally extracted his division from the clogged traffic of the Clerf valley by the mid-afternoon of 18 December. By that evening his Panzer Lehr was a mere six miles from Bastogne. Here Bayerlein faced a choice. He

could turn south to gain a hard surfaced road or could use secondary roads to avoid possible enemy roadblocks. Although he did not know it, no organized defenders guarded either route. Misled by a farmer, Bayerlein led his advanced guard along the side road. It quickly dissolved into a muddy cart path. Bayerlein spent four hours travelling an unopposed three miles to Mageret. There another Belgian told him that a large American force commanded by a major general had just passed through. Knowing such an officer commanded a full division, Bayerlein turned cautious, halted, planted a minefield and waited for dawn. This was hardly the aggressive leadership expected of a spearhead armoured division commander.

The Roadblock Battles

A combination of chance and German blunders had preserved Bastogne and allowed American reinforcements to win the race to the crossroads by the narrowest margin. About 4pm on 18 December, Colonel William Roberts arrived at the head of his CCA/10th Armored Division. This was one of the units Eisenhower had directed to come to Middleton's help back on the evening of 16 December. Middleton wanted Roberts to form three task forces to block three routes leading to the town. 'That's no way to use armour,' objected Roberts. 'Robbie,' replied Middleton, 'I may not know as much about the employment of armour as you, but that's the way I have to use them. . . Move with the utmost speed. And Robbie, hold these positions at all costs.' Again American armour was being deployed in penny packets to form hasty roadblocks. Two teams went east; Team Cherry to Longvilly and Team O'Hara to Wardin, while the third moved north-east to Noville. With Roberts still present, Middleton received another visitor, the acting commander of the 101st Airborne Division, Brigadier General Anthony McAuliffe. Knowing neither the situation nor where his unit was bound, on his own initiative McAuliffe had sped ahead to confer with Middleton. Forcing his way through the westwards-fleeing traffic, McAuliffe had become alarmed. Middleton's calm appraisal hardly reassured him: 'There has been a

▶ *Still exuberant in the advance, German soldiers ride forward on a panzer's deck. (US National Archives)*

The counter to blitzkrieg was defence in depth. By small-unit initiative and stubborn refusal to retreat, the US defenders unwittingly achieved a defence in depth. Unaware as to events on either flank, many units held at critical road junctions. This forced the attackers to use secondary tracks and to infiltrate through the woods in order to bypass the defenders and head west. Frequently they then encountered reserve formations – supply and service troops, artillery and anti-aircraft personnel, engineers and headquarters units. The willingness of these rear-area formations to use their abundant weapons and mobility gave the Americans a deep defence. Note the shot-up windscreen on this jeep. (Charles B. MacDonald Collection, US Army Military History Institute) ▶

major penetration. Certain of my units, especially the 106th and 28th Divisions, are broken.' McAuliffe's 101st would be diverted to Bastogne and hold the key road junction against all comers.

19 December was the last day during which the Germans stood any chance of seizing Bastogne by coup de main. If so, the blow would have to be delivered by the Panzer Lehr Division. At 5.30am, Bayerlein ordered his panzers to advance on Neffe, a village just east of Bastogne. His advance guard reached the village at 7am and then inexplicably halted for an hour. This delay cost Bayerlein his final chance to capture Bastogne before the 101st Airborne intervened.

◀ *German gunners swab the barrel of their 75mm anti-tank gun outside Bastogne while panzers and infantry advance nearby. This is another sketch by the 26th VGD anti-tank gunner. (Charles B. MacDonald Collection, US Army Military History Institute)*

◀ *The converging German attack destroyed Team Cherry. Bastogne could have fallen to both the Panzer Lehr and the 2nd Panzer Divisions. Von Manteuffel later blamed Bayerlein for failing to act independently and thus capturing Bastogne. He committed 'a breach in the regulations applying to the leadership of a panzer division'. Yet von Manteuffel explained his own decision to order the 2nd Panzer to ignore Bastogne as justified on the basis of the need to adhere to the plan. (US Army Military History Institute)*

In a further example of the tremendous value of unchallenged air supremacy, the 101st Airborne had raced much of the way to Bastogne aboard trucks displaying full headlights – an unmistakeable target to hostile aircraft had there been any. McAuliffe again conferred with Middleton. The paratroop general had to decide what to do amid an extremely fluid situation without having access to hard information. In characteristic Airborne style, he aggressively sent the first unit to arrive, the 501st Parachute Infantry Regiment, east. The regiment's advanced battalion collided with the Germans at Neffe. What in reality was an encounter skirmish was misperceived by both sides. The paratroopers thought they had struck an enemy roadblock. The Germans believed that they faced a combined-arms counterattack. German tanks, to which the lightly armed paratroopers had no answer, prevented further American advance. The 501st extended its lines to probe for a German weakness. Meanwhile it called on its rapid-firing light howitzers to shell Neffe.

Unfamiliar with this weapon's sound, Bayerlein believed he was hearing American heavy tank fire. Thinking he faced a large counterattack, and worried about the American armour to his rear on the Longvilly road (Team Cherry, one of Roberts' roadblocks), Bayerlein lost his nerve. Up to this point, the Germans had been encountering small, disorganized units during their race to Bastogne. Collision with formed, aggressive infantry threw them off their stride. Shortly after the war Bayerlein explained: 'The movement of the infantry regiment which had come out of Bastogne to attack me had reacted decisively on my thinking.' S.L.A. Marshal puts it more succinctly. By the advance on Neffe: 'a few American platoons hardened the fate of armies.'

By mid-afternoon, 19 December, German generals from XLVII Panzer Corps down felt that Bastogne could not be captured without committing the entire corps to the effort. For the remainder of the day, German efforts east of Bastogne focused on the elimination of Team Cherry.

The team had been struggling to extricate itself since morning. Its vehicles had become intermixed with elements of CCR/9th Armored fleeing back to Bastogne. When Team Cherry tried to turn around, its lead Sherman fell victim to a German anti-tank gun. Then two anti-aircraft half-tracks, attached to CCR/9th, had raced to the front of the column in an effort to escape. Heedless of shouts to stop, they rounded a curve, spotted the burning tank, and bailed out to avoid a crash. The resultant pile-up plugged the narrow road leading back to Bastogne. At this point three German columns converged on Team Cherry and opened fire.

On the 19th, after destroying the Longvilly roadblock, Luttwitz suggested using his entire corps to capture Bastogne. Von Manteuffel could not believe the Americans would risk annihilation and let themselves become surrounded. Calculating that he could capture Bastogne by default, he adhered to his primary mission and ordered Luttwitz to leave Bastogne for the infantry, to follow the plan and continue west. It was a key mistake.

Trapped motionless, Team Cherry disintegrated under the plunging German fire. Its long column of light tanks, tank destroyers, ambulances and armoured cars filled the air with oily black smoke as one vehicle after another was hit. The team fought back when it could and managed to knock out eight German tanks. But by and large the helpless crews and accompanying infantry could do nothing more than line the ditches, endure and wait for darkness. The action on the Longvilly road saw the virtual destruction of the remnant of CCR/9th Armored, including its entire armoured field artillery battalion. Team Cherry lost 175 officers and men, a quarter of its command, along with seven light, ten medium tanks, and seventeen half-tracks. Substantial elements of other units were also caught in the Longvilly trap. Yet the Americans had absorbed the attention of a German corps and two German divisional generals along with elements from two panzer divisions when all should have been focusing on other objectives.

Summarizing events through the offensive's first three days, the perceptive commentator Pimlott writes that by the end of the 19th: 'The period of American confusion, during which the major German advances should have been made, was already coming to an end.'

THE DEFENCE OF ST VITH

Surrender on the Schnee Eifel

Like Bastogne, St Vith was a key road net and a potential bottleneck. Also like Bastogne, with an ample panzer force at hand German planners had assigned an infantry unit for its capture. This unit, the 18th VGD, first had to form one of the pincers around the Schnee Eifel and then advance on St Vith. On 17 December, St Vith was open to a coup de main since few defenders were in place. But the 18th lacked the mobility for such a coup. Its mobile battalion, comprising three assault gun platoons, a company of engineers and another of fusiliers, was inadequate to accomplish the task. Jodl and his OKW planners again had committed

a capital blunder by failing to match force and mission.

The period from 17 to 19 December passed without significant pressure coming to bear against St Vith. Conversely, the Americans were unable to counterattack to relieve the defenders on the Schnee Eifel. Before dawn on 17 December CCB/9th Armored Division arrived in St Vith. The commander of the 106th Infantry Division, as senior general at St Vith, absorbed it within his command and promptly split its infantry and tank components. He sent the 27th Armored Infantry Battalion forward to attack the German force slicing around the right flank of the Schnee Eifel. The counterattack achieved nothing except to run up the casualty list until the surprise appearance of a supporting American tank platoon shook the Germans. The German reaction is an indication of what might have been had American generals used their armour en masse. Ninety German infantry surrendered in a situation the German divisional commander later referred to as a 'serious crisis'. While this and other American counterattacks helped preserve St Vith, they did not retrieve the fortunes of the isolated regiments on the Schnee Eifel.

With hopes of relief by early counterattack dashed, the Schnee Eifel defenders faced a crippling supply shortage. Aerial re-supply should have solved this problem, but the effort was badly botched. Remarkably, although Allied land forces had been on the continent for over half a year, the only supply containers prepared for parachuting remained in England. Bringing them forward in admittedly poor weather proved beyond Allied

◀ *American prisoners photographed in a German village in the Eifel area. (US National Archives)*

▶ The gun crew of a 3in tank destroyer struggles to manoeuvre it into position. (US National Archives)

capability. The two isolated regiments made a last effort to cut their way free on 19 December, but the effort collapsed in the face of withering German artillery fire. That afternoon most surviving defenders – some seven to eight thousand (the exact figure is debated to this day) – surrendered, thus bringing to a conclusion the costliest American defeat during the war in Europe and, next to Bataan, the greatest mass surrender in American history.

After the war American interrogators asked von Manteuffel a leading question: had the cut-off troops resisted as strongly as he had anticipated? Von Manteuffel answered: 'No.'

Breakwater

The German failure to advance on St Vith during the first three days allowed the defence of the St Vith-Vielsalm area to assume a recognizable form. According to the official army historian, by the night of 19 December: 'The troops within the perimeter occupied an "island" within a German tide rushing past on the north and south and rising against its eastern face.' The most advanced German troops had bypassed their position and were 25 miles south-west. The defenders were out of touch with headquarters and the command situation did not improve when, unnerved by the disintegration of his division, the 106th's commanding officer gave a lower ranking officer, General Bruce Clarke, CCA/7th Armored Division, responsibility for conducting the defence.

The commander of the 7th Armored Division, Brigadier General Robert Hasbrouck, described the situation in a letter to First Army headquarters: 'Both infantry regiments are in bad shape. My right flank is wide open except for some reconnaissance elements, TDs, and stragglers we have collected and organized into defence teams at road centres . . . I can delay them [the Germans] the rest of today maybe but will be cut off by tomorrow. VIII Corps has ordered me to hold and I will do so but need help.' Here was a remarkable display of calm determination.

St Vith also loomed large in German planning. The stubborn defence of the twin villages and the Elsenborn Ridge forced Sixth Panzer Army to shift southward to seek a route to the Meuse. Whereas Peiper could and did slip between American positions, an entire army required a road net to support its advance. On 20 December, the single free road the Germans held served as the main supply route for two armoured and two infantry divisions. All other roads west ran through St Vith. The colossal traffic jam caused by the stubborn retention of St Vith was felt all the way up the German chain of command. Both Model and von

◀ Congested roads leading to St Vith impaired the German advance and forced the top commanders to walk to their meeting. Given that the mud even bogged down light staff cars, like the one shown here, it is easy to understand why the panzers had difficulty. (US National Archives)

Manteuffel had to abandon their staff cars on the clogged roads and walk in order to arrive at a strategic planning meeting. This session between Model and von Manteuffel, army group and army commander respectively, close to the front contrasts sharply with the American operating style. Not for a lack of courage, neither Bradley nor Hodges toured the front during the critical first days.

When von Manteuffel confidently responded to Model's question about Fifth Panzer Army's progress, the latter expressed some doubt: 'I got the impression you were lagging, especially in the St Vith sector.' 'Yes,' acknowledged von Manteuffel, 'but we'll take it tomorrow.' 'I expect you to. And so that you'll take it quicker, tomorrow I'm letting you use the Führer Escort Brigade.'

The German generals expected that 20 December would see an attack featuring the forces released by the American surrender on the Schnee Eifel, the 62nd and 18th VGDs, and the fresh, powerful, Führer Begleit (Escort) Brigade commanded by Colonel Otto Remer. In the event the day passed with surprising calm. The attackers simply could not organize themselves for the assault. In particular, the horse-drawn artillery experienced great difficulty extricating batteries along muddy, forest paths and repositioning them against St Vith.

Impatient, von Manteuffel ordered Remer to attack with his advance guard, but Remer was more interested in the glory drive west than dealing with the troublesome St Vith defenders. Accordingly, Remer made a half-hearted effort. When 90mm guns of an American TD battalion knocked out his four leading Mark IVs, he disobeyed and halted his attack.

On 21 December, Remer again disregarded von Manteuffel's orders and headed west. This left St Vith to the two Volksgrenadier divisions. Their main attack came from the east and was directed against a rugged ridge known as the Prumerberg. Defending was an ad-hoc force commanded by Lieutenant Colonel William Fuller. This force included four 7th Armored Division armoured infantry companies, 400 engineers, two TD companies and 11 Sherman tanks. A 45-minute artillery barrage began the German attack in late afternoon. Tree bursts rained deadly splinters on the American foxholes. Nebelwerfers added their terrifying din. Veterans claimed it was the worst bombardment they had ever experienced. The shelling wounded a tank company commander and sent one of his platoon leaders into shock.

The German Assault, from 20 to 24 December

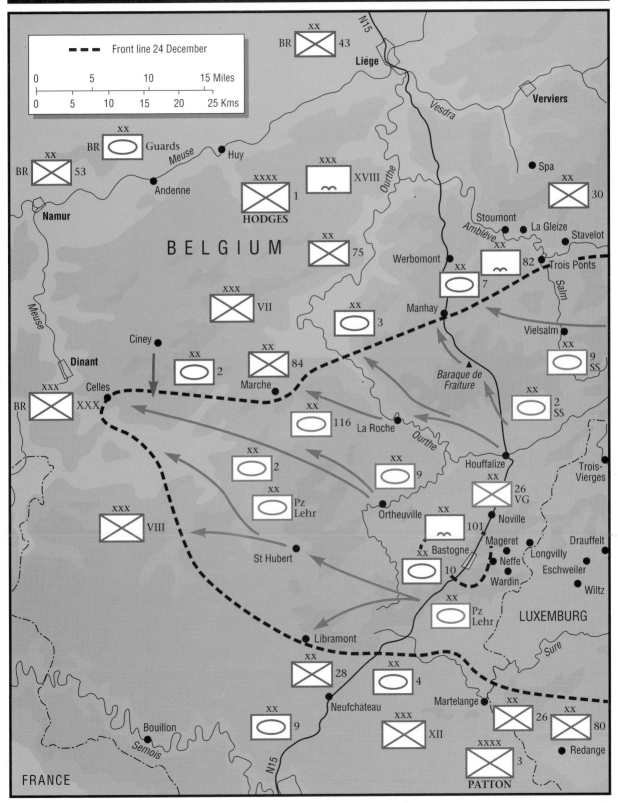

- - - Front line 24 December

0   5   10   15 Miles
0 5 10 15 20 25 Kms

BR XX 43
Liège
N15
Verviers
Vesdra
BR XX Guards
Meuse
Huy
XXX XVIII
Ourthe
Spa
BR XX 53
Andenne
XXXX 1 HODGES
XX 30
Stoumont   La Gleize   Stavelot
Amblève
Namur
BELGIUM
XX 75
Werbomont
XX 82
Trois Ponts
XX 7
Manhay
Salm
XXX VII
XX 3
Vielsalm
Meuse
Ciney
XX 2
XX 84
Marche
Baraque de Fraiture
XX 9 SS
Dinant
XXX BR XXX
Celles
XX 116
La Roche
Ourthe
XX 2 SS
XX 2
XX 9
Houffalize
Trois-Vierges
XX Pz Lehr
Ortheuville
XX 26 VG
Noville
XXX VIII
XX 101
Magaret   Drauffelt
XX Bastogne
Neffe   Longvilly   Eschweiler
St Hubert
XX 10
Wardin   Wiltz
XX Pz Lehr
LUXEMBURG
Libramont
Sure
XX 28
XX 4
Martelange
Bouillon
XX 9
Neufchateau
XXX XII
XX 26
XX 80
Redange
Semois
N15
XXXX 3 PATTON
FRANCE

63

At dusk the German infantry advanced. American artillery severely punished them, breaking up one entire regimental assault. The German commander threw everything he had into the attack. Infantry skilfully infiltrated gaps in the American line and began roaming the rear to isolate the forward defenders. In near darkness six SS Tigers rolled up the front slopes of the Prumerberg. Blocking their advance were five Shermans. The Americans positioned their tanks beneath the crestline. The commander ordered them to fire simultaneously when the Tigers appeared over the crest. Using an Eastern Front tactic, the Tigers fired flares as they reached the crest. These blinded the American tank crews and silhouetted the Shermans. In seconds the big 88mm guns fired and destroyed all five Shermans at no cost to themselves. Then they began to shoot up the

◄ *CCA/7th Armored Division fought the all-important delaying action at St Vith. Here a white-camouflaged Sherman and its infantry escort manoeuvre through the woods. (US Army Military History Institute)*

Traffic jams that afflicted the German advance around St Vith also delayed American reinforcements. Rushing to reinforce the defenders, a tank general of the 7th Armored Division took five hours to fight through rearward flowing traffic to travel from Vielsalm to St Vith, a distance of some 10 miles. Once CCA/7th Armored arrived, it dug-in and delayed the German advance. Here machine-gunners man a snow-encrusted .30-calibre Browning. (US National ◄ *Archives)*

American foxhole line. The defending infantry had no counter and broke to the rear. Some adjacent units held; others, in the words of the official historian, 'stampeded blindly through the woods in search of an exit to the west'.

Overcome by the attack, Fuller panicked, turned over command to an engineer officer and fled to headquarters 'to plan alternate positions'. Hard on his heels, spearheaded by the Tigers, the intrepid Volksgrenadiers rolled into St Vith. In the town all was confusion, with German and American soldiers and vehicles intermingled. A heavy nocturnal snowstorm began. An artilleryman radioed headquarters for orders. 'Go West! Go West!' came the reply. In a chaotic situation ripe for panic, St Vith's commander, Clarke, coolly led the withdrawal and managed to improvise a new defensive line 1,000 yards behind the town. Converging from several directions, the advancing Germans became hopelessly entangled in St Vith's streets. Men broke ranks to seek warmth, shelter, and to loot the abundant American supplies. Thus, there was no pursuit. So clogged were the roads leading to St Vith that once again Model had to abandon his car and walk.

Afterwards the Americans could compile only partial casualty lists. The 7th Armored Division and 14th Cavalry Group listed 3,397 casualties. In addition, the armoured division lost 59 Shermans, 29 light tanks and 25 armoured cars. Against these losses must be measured their accomplishment. Again the words of the official historian: 'They had met an entire German corps flushed with easy victory and halted it in its tracks. They had firmly choked one of the main enemy lines of communication and forced days of delay on the western movement of troops, guns, tanks, and supplies belonging to two German armies.'

The American success on the Elsenborn ridge had prevented a German advance to the Meuse via the shortest route. The second best path was Route N15, which ran from Bastogne through Manhay, Werbomont and on to Liège. Without possession of Bastogne, this route became feasible only with the capture of St Vith. But St Vith's fall proved too late for the Germans. The American defence had time to consolidate across the projected path of advance. Further advance would require tough fighting with exhausted troops. In the event the German conquerors of St Vith could not exploit their victory. Further success hinged upon the conduct of those forces that had earlier bypassed this pocket of resistance and advanced along portions of Route 15.

There was a 13-mile gap between the American outposts behind St Vith and the Bastogne perimeter. If the German units rolling through this gap could join the most advanced spearheads, together they could crack the American flank bending back from St Vith to Malmédy and Manhay. Then they could continue west. Since a substantial portion of the American strength was involved in checking Peiper, the American line along this front was thin, with defences as yet uncoordinated. Henceforth, the battle featured a race to acquire key road junctions and river crossings leading to the Meuse.

▼ *Formerly charged with providing anti-aircraft defence for Hitler's headquarters, the Führer Begleit Brigade comprised a flak regiment with 24 88mm guns (shown here on the Eastern front), three mobile grenadier battalions, a 105mm artillery battalion, a panzer battalion with 45 Mark IVs and 35 assault guns, plus anti-tank and engineer attachments. In a manner typical of many German élite formations, its commander proved disobedient to army directives, preferring his personal, glory-seeking agenda. Von Manteuffel felt that committing this formidable reserve unit, which was intended to exploit a breakthrough, at St Vith instead of in support of his spearhead elements was a major blunder. (Wood Collection, US Army Military History Institute)*

▲Congested roads placed a premium on traffic control. Aided by air supremacy, the Americans generally out-performed the Germans in this overlooked but important function. Here a victim of too much haste, an M-36 TD has slipped on an icy road and overturned. (US National Archives)

▲The paratroopers of the 82nd and 101st Airborne were the best soldiers in the American Army. They were much more aggressive than line infantry. Here gunners of the 101st man a 3in anti-tank weapon, the barrel of which is camouflaged with fence posts. (US National Archives)

THE DEFENCE OF BASTOGNE

Command Decisions

The Supreme Allied Commander had been watching the Ardennes situation unfold with growing alarm. On the evening of 19 December he convened an emergency meeting that featured decisions vitally affecting Bastogne's fate. On the situation map it appeared that Peiper had achieved a clean breakthrough. Other enemy forces were racing through the gap between Bastogne and St Vith. Rising to the occasion, Eisenhower struck exactly the right note with his opening remarks: 'The present situation is to be regarded as one of opportunity for us and not of disaster. There will be only cheerful faces at this conference table.'

Patton boldly replied: 'Hell, let's have the guts

◄ *Artillery provided Bastogne's defensive backbone. A participant observed a German assault: 'Here and there, among the mushrooming clouds of artillery smoke, the tiny black figures stumbled and fell. Behind them one of the heavy tanks turned back towards its own lines – then rolled and halted . . . The tiny figures of the Germans began to run. More and more of them fell. For twenty minutes the rolling barrage continued to pursue them. When it lifted, the only Germans who remained on the open field were the scores of still bodies.' Here knocked out German vehicles and a dead panzergrenadier lie outside Bastogne. (US National Archives)*

to let the sons of bitches go all the way to Paris. Then we'll really cut 'em up and chew 'em up.' Patton's astonishing, but none the less insightful suggestion had much merit. It would fully capitalize on the great American asset of mobility. It meshed with Bradley's original scheme calling for a fighting withdrawal. But Eisenhower and Bradley typically preferred a more cautious approach.

Ike responded to Patton: 'No, the enemy will never be allowed to cross the Meuse.' His plan was American textbook doctrine based on the lessons of the First World War: firmly hold the shoulders of the penetration. The rush west would be slowed by blocking the road hubs at St Vith and Bastogne while defences were manned behind the Meuse. A major counterattack would be launched as soon as possible.

Hodges' battered units could not participate, so everything hinged on Patton. Eisenhower asked him: 'When can you attack?' Before attending the meeting Patton had carefully examined the situation and had drawn up three contingency attack plans. Consequently, he confidently answered: 'On December 22, with three divisions.'

Patton's bravado irked Eisenhower. In any event he did not particularly like Patton and, not knowing Patton had already considered the problem in detail, believed that this was a typical flippant answer to a serious question. Furthermore, he doubted anyone could turn his army 90 degrees, make an approach march in winter against the grain of his communications and strike the German flank. After dressing down the Third Army commander, Eisenhower authorized a delay of 24-48 extra hours to prepare the attack.

Belying Ike's contempt, as soon as he departed the meeting, Patton telephoned his headquarters to speak in pre-arranged code to his staff. His message informed them which offensive option to employ. According to Patton's biographer, his response to Eisenhower's question was 'the sublime moment of his career'.

Unaware of these decisions, von Manteuffel claimed that on the night of 19 December 'serious doubts arose for the first time' as to the ultimate success of his Fifth Army's operations.

The Ordeal Begins

By 20 December all the units that were to defend Bastogne were in place. Smaller than a conventional infantry division, the 101st Airborne had 11,840 men divided into four infantry regiments. This 'square' formation better lent itself to four-sided defence than the more common three-regiment structure. Three battalions of light, 75mm pack howitzers (the type that had fooled Bayerlein) and one standard 105mm battalion provided the organic artillery support. The other major defending unit was Robert's CCB/10th Armored Division already deployed into task forces to block important roads. By day's end CCB had some 30 medium tanks left. The remnant of CCR/9th Armored probably contributed another 10 Shermans. The 705th Tank Destroyer Battalion armed with new, high-velocity 76mm guns, gave the defenders 36 self-propelled TDs. Also present were four corps artillery battalions whose 155mm howitzers provided McAuliffe (who, after all, was formally his division's artillery commander) long-range firepower. About 130 artillery tubes were inside Bastogne. In addition, the defenders had numerous stragglers and partial units which had filtered back to Bastogne during the chaotic first days. McAuliffe positioned his men along a circular perimeter centred on Bastogne with his artillery centrally grouped to fire in any direction.

On the night of 20 December, McAuliffe visited Middleton in Neufchâteau. He told Middleton that he was certain his men could hold on for at least 48 hours if they became surrounded. The VIII Corps commander apprised him of the latest intelligence, including news that the 116th Panzer Division appeared to be coming in on McAuliffe's flank to add to the three divisions already attacking Bastogne. McAuliffe replied: 'I think we can take care of them.' The airborne commander returned to Bastogne. Some 30 minutes later, German armour cut the road behind him. Bastogne was isolated.

'Nuts!'

Bastogne's isolation came about because of a change in German tactics. Having been stopped cold at Neffe, and unable to slip into Bastogne via

◀ The Bastogne defenders fought with a special determination. A 10th Armored soldier entered a building to see a hand-scrawled message on the wall left by a departing VIII Corps soldier. It read: 'We'll be back – The Yanks.' The reader snorted: 'We'll be back – Hell! We're here to stay.' Here a foxhole with a .50-calibre machine-gun removed from a vehicle and a bazooka (to right of machine-gun) defends the perimeter. The freshly turned earth against the white background provides an unmistakeable target. (US National Archives)

▶ *A colonel on the ground, witnessing the pilots of these C-47s flying straight and level amid heavy anti-aircraft fire so as to deliver their supply bundles accurately, commented: 'Their courage was tremendous, and I believe that their example did a great deal to encourage my infantry.' (US Air Force photograph; print from Military Archive & Research Services)*

Marvie, the Germans concluded that they lacked the strength to capture Bastogne. Instead, they decided to encircle the town. The next two days, 21-2 December, witnessed numerous probes but no full-scale combat, as the Germans manoeuvred around Bastogne's perimeter. This respite gave McAuliffe invaluable time to knit together his paratroopers and armour, who previously had cooperated in uneasy alliance, each arm believing that they alone carried the burden of defence.

At 11.30am on 22 December, four Germans approached the American outpost line carrying a large white flag. Their appearance triggered one of the most memorable incidents of the Battle of the Bulge. They carried a paper demanding Bastogne's surrender and threatening dire consequences if the garrison failed to do so. When the surrender demand reached McAuliffe he laughed and said: 'Aw, nuts!' He believed his men were giving the attackers 'one hell of a beating' and that the demand was ridiculously inappropriate. He sat down to draft a written response and came up blank.

He asked his staff what they thought and one officer replied: 'That first remark of yours would be hard to beat.' So the Germans received the celebrated one word answer, 'Nuts!' But the untranslatable reply was not understood by the German negotiators. An American colonel assisted: 'If you don't understand what "Nuts" means, in plain English it is the same as "Go to hell". And I will tell you something else – if you continue to attack we will kill every goddam German that tries to break into this city.'

Although the defenders' spirits were undaunted, they now faced a serious matériel problem – ammunition. For the first three days Bastogne's ample artillery had decisively intervened whenever a massed target appeared. As elsewhere in the Ardennes, American artillery provided the defensive backbone. By midday on 22 December, McAuliffe had to restrict artillery fire severely in order to conserve ammunition. Guns received a ten round per day ration. This allowed the Germans to manoeuvre openly all around Bastogne's perimeter. The paratroopers were also running low on small-arms ammunition. Everyone wondered if ammunition would give out before relief came.

The day before the airdrop, McAuliffe received a brief, encouraging radio message: 'Hugh [General Gaffey of Patton's 4th Armored Division] is coming.' This manoeuvre was part of the promised Third Army counterattack. The Third Army advanced along a broad front between Echternach and Martelange. German planners had assigned Seventh Army the role of providing flank protection against exactly this type of attack. However, the counterattack came much sooner than the Germans had expected. None the less, difficult terrain and tenacious resistance led to as grim a fight as occurred during the entire battle and slowed Patton's advance to a crawl.

The highly regarded 4th Armored Division had been assigned the mission of relieving Bastogne. During the breakout from Normandy, led by a superb commander, the 4th Armored had earned a reputation for slashing attacks and had become Patton's favourite. But in late December, one of Patton's former staff officers, Gaffey, led the unit. Many of its tanks were the same vehicles that had

crossed France and were thus mechanically unreliable. All too many vehicles were being driven by replacement crews. Originally one of the division's combat commands had been well-positioned at Neufchâteau to attack towards Bastogne, but a command foul-up led to a counter-march and forced the division to attack towards Martelange. In spite of Patton's urgings to 'drive like hell', the 4th was making slow progress.

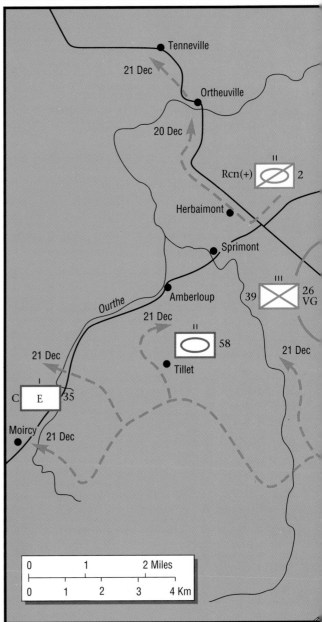

The Defence of Bastogne

▲ *The élite 4th Armored Division began its drive to relieve Bastogne without its superb commander, with ranks only partially replenished with green soldiers, and driving tanks issued in England before D-Day. Some ran only at medium speed, others had turrets without electrical traverse, and most had worn motors and tracks. One tank battalion lost 33 tanks to mechanical failure during its 160-mile rush to the Ardennes. On 24* *December, Patton wrote in his diary: 'This has been a very bad Christmas Eve. All along our line we have received violent counterattacks, one of which forced . . . the 4th Armored back.' None the less, Patton concluded that the Germans 'are far behind schedule and, I believe, beaten'. This illustration shows a white-camouflaged 4th Armored Division tank. (US Army Military History Institute)*

Inside Bastogne the defenders felt let down. 'Hugh' simply was not coming fast enough. Small tank-infantry teams were continually striking the perimeter and beginning to wear the defenders down. 23 December dawned bright and clear. The Ninth Air Force's medium B-26 bombers and P-38 and P-47 fighter-bombers dominated the day. An observer saw them 'like shoals of silver minnows in the bright winter sun'. The 'Jabos' hunted for tell-tale vehicle tracks in the snow and followed them to the target. Generally, the German vehicles sheltered in the numerous small woods. The 'Jabos' used rockets, bombs and napalm to ferret them out. During the day the Ninth flew close to 1,300 sorties.

Better than the combat aircraft was the arrival of the lumbering transport aircraft. With practised skill, pathfinders parachuted into Bastogne in the

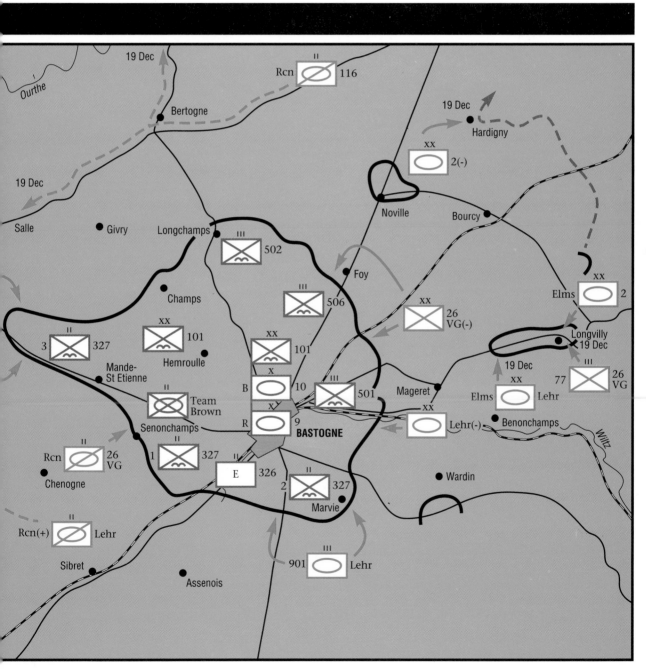

◄ *Veteran American tank crews feared German anti-tank guns more than tanks. They felt they would usually hear or see opposing tanks. They seldom saw an anti-tank gun until it opened fire. This sketch by the 26th VGD gunner shows why; his 75mm gun is in perfect enfilade as US half-tracks pass his sights on 24 December. He failed to knock the target out. (Charles B. MacDonald Collection, US Army Military History Institute)*

morning of 23 December and set up radar to direct incoming C-47s. During the day 241 aircraft dropped their supply bundles with great precision. Ground forces recovered 95 per cent of these supplies. The next day the transports returned, but this time the Germans were ready for them. While the Germans' fierce anti-aircraft fire knocked down a number of C-47s, the pilots refused to take evasive action so as to deliver accurately the precious supplies. Their gallantry delivered Bastogne from perhaps its severest crisis.

At 3am on Christmas Day, the Germans delivered an all-out attack against Bastogne. The assault was supposed to feature an entire fresh division, the 15th Panzergrenadier. Instead only two panzergrenadier battalions, two self-propelled artillery battalions and eighteen tanks arrived in time. The 15th PGD colonel who commanded the assault force protested that he had been given no time for reconnaissance and that he had been unable to coordinate with his panzer supports. German planning regarding Bastogne was beginning to take on a desperate urgency. Model had ordered Fifth Panzer Army to seize Bastogne at once to 'lance this boil'. Consequently, the colonel's superiors replied that he must attack and should count on the tremendous advantage of

surprise since the Americans would be celebrating Christmas.

Elements of the 15th PGD joined infantry from the 26th VGD and attacked west of Bastogne at Champs. The assault plan called for the attackers to enter Bastogne between 8 and 9am, before the fighter-bombers appeared. Following initial success, by 10am Kokott knew his plan was doomed. He requested permission to withdraw, but his corps commander refused, saying it was vital to capture Bastogne. Reluctantly, Kokott persisted. He knew further effort would only increase the butcher's bill. So the Christmas Day attack against Bastogne petered out. As at Neffe on 19 December, the Germans had penetrated to within one mile of Bastogne. They would never get closer.

Meanwhile, south-west of Bastogne, the US CCR/4th Armored Division faced demolished bridges, cratered roads and tough German resistance as it drove towards the town. By late afternoon the command's leaders doubted whether they could break through if they followed the prescribed route of advance. They asked permission to try a short-cut. The division passed the request up to Patton, asking if he would authorize a bold venture that risked a German flank attack. Patton responded: 'I sure as hell will!'

In CCR's van was a lieutenant colonel destined to make a name for himself. Twenty-eight years in the future, Creighton Abrams would become supreme ground commander of the US forces in Vietnam. Outside Bastogne, he commanded a mere under-strength battalion with 20 Shermans, but he was determined to make the most of it. Sticking a cigar in his mouth he told his command: 'We're going in now. Let 'er roll!'

Leading the way were a handful of the new, upgraded 40-tonne Sherman tanks called Cobra Kings. Hard on the heels of a brief but intense artillery bombardment, Abrams charged into Assenois. Leaping from aboard the tanks, infantry cleared the village in bitter house-to-house fighting. None surpassed a 19-year old private, James Hendrix. Armed with only a rifle, Hendrix attacked two 88mm anti-tank guns. 'Come on out!' he shouted. A German soldier lifted his head from a foxhole and Hendrix shot him. Running to the next hole, Hendrix clubbed its occupant with his rifle butt. Then he charged straight at the two big guns. Dismayed by this beserker-like warrior display, the crews surrendered. It was a one-man assault worthy of the Medal of Honor it won.

Propelled by such valour, the Cobra Kings sped on. They broke through to the 101st's lines, where McAuliffe greeted them: 'Gee, I am mighty glad to see you.' Bastogne's 'siege' was over.

▲ *The Americans had some upgraded Shermans called 'Cobra Kings' armed with 76mm guns with muzzle brakes and having thicker frontal armour. Patton ordered that they lead the effort to break through to Bastogne. (US Army Military History Institute)*

▼ *Armoured infantry of 4th Armored Division attack to widen the corridor into Bastogne on 27 December. The men are widely dispersed to limit casualties in case they are shelled. (US Army Military History Institute)*

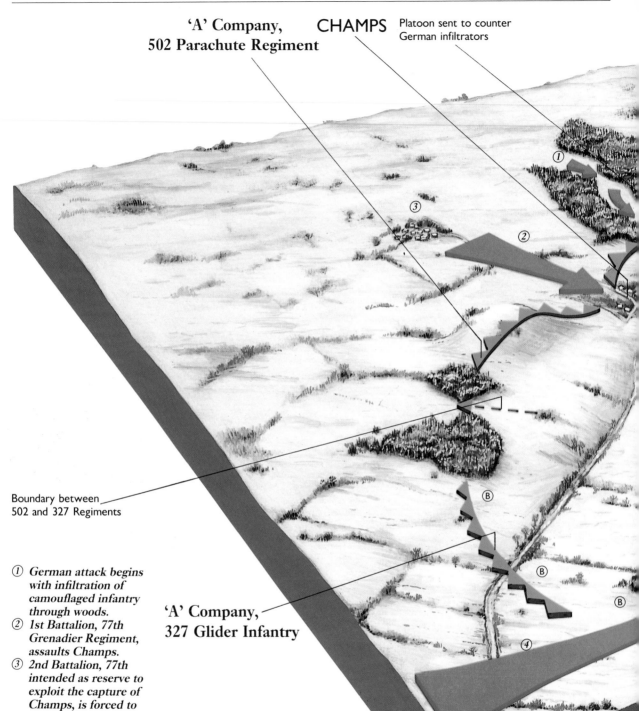

'A' Company, 502 Parachute Regiment

CHAMPS

Platoon sent to counter German infiltrators

Boundary between 502 and 327 Regiments

'A' Company, 327 Glider Infantry

① German attack begins with infiltration of camouflaged infantry through woods.

② 1st Battalion, 77th Grenadier Regiment, assaults Champs.

③ 2nd Battalion, 77th intended as reserve to exploit the capture of Champs, is forced to join house-to-house combat when US 'A' Company puts up stubborn resistance.

④ German main attack with 18 panzers rolls over foxhole line, brushes aside US tank-destroyers and advances on Bastogne.

⑤ German attack splits: half the force drives on Rolle, half on Hemroulle.

⑥ Panzers destroy two tank-destroyers fleeing from Champs.

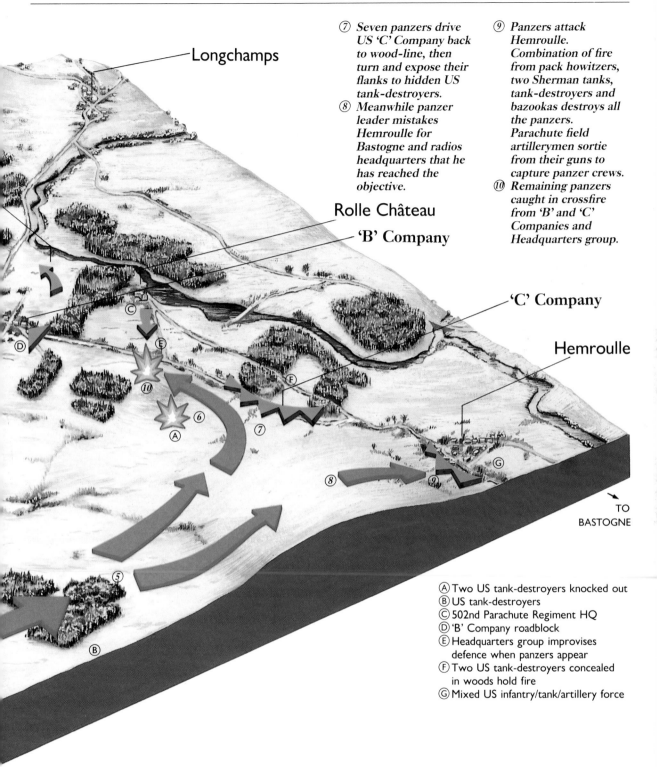

⑦ Seven panzers drive US 'C' Company back to wood-line, then turn and expose their flanks to hidden US tank-destroyers.

⑧ Meanwhile panzer leader mistakes Hemroulle for Bastogne and radios headquarters that he has reached the objective.

⑨ Panzers attack Hemroulle. Combination of fire from pack howitzers, two Sherman tanks, tank-destroyers and bazookas destroys all the panzers. Parachute field artillerymen sortie from their guns to capture panzer crews.

⑩ Remaining panzers caught in crossfire from 'B' and 'C' Companies and Headquarters group.

Longchamps

Rolle Château

'B' Company

'C' Company

Hemroulle

TO BASTOGNE

Ⓐ Two US tank-destroyers knocked out
Ⓑ US tank-destroyers
Ⓒ 502nd Parachute Regiment HQ
Ⓓ 'B' Company roadblock
Ⓔ Headquarters group improvises defence when panzers appear
Ⓕ Two US tank-destroyers concealed in woods hold fire
Ⓖ Mixed US infantry/tank/artillery force

THE BATTLE FOR CHAMPS

25 December 1944.

TO THE MEUSE

The Drive Falters

When the 2nd Panzer Division's advance guards captured a bridge over the Ourthe at Ortheuville on 21 December, they stood less than 40 road miles from Dinant and the Meuse. Before embarking on a final sprint to the Meuse, von Manteuffel had to solve several problems. The 2nd's spearhead was extremely narrow, extending no further than the range of its 75mm tank guns. Part of his left panzer corps was stuck at Bastogne; elements of his right had to conduct time-consuming counter-marches because of American opposition. When the Panzer Lehr and 116th Panzer Divisions came up on the left and right respectively, von Manteuffel would have sufficient force for a broad-based advance to the Meuse. Even then, he would have to leave forces behind to guard his northern flank with each mile he advanced west. All his units were tired, having fought without rest for six solid days. Fatigue's consequences would be seen the next day when the 2nd Panzer's main column halted upon rumour of American tanks. The corps commander hastened to the front, relieved the colonel in command, sent in fresh troops, and the advance resumed – but valuable hours had been lost. Finally, and as it turned out most importantly, fuel deliveries to the forward elements were not getting through. Already major manoeuvre elements had been immobilized for lack of it.

Von Manteuffel's drive to the Meuse was a consequence of decisions made higher in the chain of command. As early as 18 December, Model had phoned von Rundstedt and Jodl to say the offensive had failed. By 24 December he hoped that the 2nd Panzer Division's position could be used to trap and destroy American forces against the Meuse – a return to the 'small solution'. Von Rundstedt was even more pessimistic. On Christ-

mas Day he requested that the attack be halted since even the 'small solution' was now impossible. According to an officer at Hitler's headquarters: 'In spite of all this Hitler not merely clung to the major plan but began to toy with even more ambitious ideas.'

Regardless of von Manteuffel's plans to broaden the 2nd Panzer Division's spearhead and to open a wider supporting road net, during 22-4 December the westernmost elements of Fifth Panzer Army achieved little. Much of the problem was due to the inability of the neighbouring Sixth Panzer Army to create a blocking line east of Liège. It had tried to slip past the Elsenborn position, but American artillery interdicted nearby east-west roads, leaving the remaining roads clogged with traffic. Typical was the experience of the 9th SS Panzer Division: committed on 18 December as part of the second wave, it did not reach the front until four days later. Consequently, Sixth Panzer Army failed to develop the momentum and achieve room to manoeuvre sufficient to perform its blocking mission. Left to its own resources, Fifth Panzer Army's advance slowed to a crawl. Such was its sorry state – its spearhead scattered all the way back to Bastogne, its most advanced units without fuel – that on 24 December Model ordered its advance guard 'to proceed on foot' to the Meuse. The dream of a blitzkrieg had died.

Change of Command

On 20 December, Eisenhower made a decision that shocked senior American generals. He divided American forces into northern and southern components. Those to the north were to be commanded by Field Marshal Montgomery. Ike's controversial decision stemmed from Montgomery's own suggestion to divide the battlefield. Bradley's stubborn refusal to relocate his headquarters rearward once the Germans penetrated between his First and Third Armies played right into Monty's hands. SHAEF staff planners worried that the German advance imperilled Bradley's communications with First Army. Noting that his headquarters had never retreated, Bradley claimed the resultant loss of prestige associated with its first retreat might instil panic in his men. This belief exhibits a ridiculous lack of confidence in his men and inappropriate concern with an unimportant symbol. Had Bradley been less stiff necked, much trouble could have been avoided because Montgomery planned to use the American setback to renew his campaign to become supreme land general of the Allied forces. In his memoirs, Bradley acknowledged that consenting to the command change was 'one of my biggest mistakes of the war'.

The Americans believed a second good reason for putting Monty in charge was that it would hasten British reinforcements to the front. While Montgomery did quickly bring his excellent XXX Corps to the River Meuse, once there it merely provided rear-area security and hardly became engaged. The entire battle cost the British slightly more than 200 killed. In addition to the crisis in command that stemmed from Ike's 20 December decision, a second important consequence was that Montgomery permitted his self-justifying argument for one overall ground commander to colour his view of the strategic opportunities for American counterattack.

Montgomery arrived at Hodges' headquarters, according to a British observer, 'like Christ come to cleanse the Temple'. He ordered the Americans to withdraw to straighten their lines. Giving up ground was outside the American experience. Hodges argued against yielding an inch. For the time being Monty demurred. But he soon became convinced that he should sack Hodges. Indeed, SHAEF had lost confidence in Hodges, who was admittedly exhausted after four exceedingly tough days. Ike retained confidence in Hodges, an opinion bolstered by the fact that even at this moment Hodges planned a counterattack at the base of the German penetration. Coupled with Patton's attack, the dual pincers had the chance of cutting off the bulk of the German forces still involved in a struggle to reach the Meuse. Montgomery preferred the more cautious approach of 'tidying up' the battlefield before counterattacking.

Last Crisis on the Ground

While the American withdrawal from the St Vith area took place on the night of 23 December, the 82nd Airborne defended a 15-mile long sector blocking the German advance towards Liège. It was a poorly sited position, one which the 82nd had manned by circumstance rather than design. On 24 December, Montgomery arrived at XVIII Airborne Corps headquarters to order a 'tidying' of the front. The Americans typically argued vehemently, explaining that the 82nd had never retreated in its history and should not begin now. In one of his most important positive contributions to the battle, Montgomery demanded a withdrawal north to a better position. Here was military science displayed by a master grand tactician overcoming the unthinking, bulldog tenacity that characterized most American combat decisions. When a ferocious German attack hit the 82nd two days later, it was repulsed after bitter fighting. The outcome would have been different had not Monty insisted upon the retreat.

Decisively blocked at the Elsenborn Ridge and with Peiper's spearhead lost, on 20 December Model had changed Sixth Panzer Army's mission. Henceforth Fifth Panzer Army would make the main effort and the Sixth would be relegated to providing flank protection. Model sent the uncommitted II SS Panzer Corps forward in pursuit of this mission. By the night of 22 December, American patrols had captured an SS officer and learned that an attack on Baraque de Fraiture, on the main road between Houffalize and Manhay, was forthcoming.

General James Gavin, commander of the 82nd, worried that if the Germans seized the crossroads they could drive up the highway and trap both the 82nd and the troops evacuating St Vith against the angle formed by the Rivers Amblève and Salm. Gavin went to the crossroads, realized the position's weakness, and sent his only reserve, the 2nd Battalion/325 Glider Infantry.

Following a night of heavy snow, at dawn on 23 December, SS panzergrenadiers attacked Baraque de Fraiture. The attack caught the defenders carelessly inside the buildings eating breakfast. The glider commander led a counterattack to restore the position. The next hours passed with German mortar and artillery fire shelling the crossroads. Alarmed, the glidermen asked for help. From Manhay came a platoon of Shermans, a platoon of armoured infantry belonging to the 3rd Armored Division and a company of paratroopers from a separate parachute infantry battalion. They ran into a German roadblock that forced the infantry to dismount. The five Shermans 'buttoned up' and drove through the road-block to arrive at the crossroads at 1pm. Three hours later, following a 20-minute artillery barrage, the 2nd SS Panzer Division delivered a powerful attack.

With the fall of Baraque de Fraiture, the route to Liège, Sixth Panzer Army's formal objective, lay open. Gavin scraped together what he could to block the road. Mostly they were the battered, exhausted St Vith survivors. Whether they could have held is unknown, for the Germans did not press their advantage. A break in the weather the next day allowed the 'Jabos' to dominate. The victors at the crossroads, the 2nd SS Panzer Division, had to hide in the woods. This was the first day the Germans had use of the St Vith road

Late on Christmas night, Hitler held a far-reaching staff discussion. After reviewing Model's report, Jodl paused and then spoke: 'Mein Führer, we must face the facts squarely and openly. We cannot force the Meuse River.' The photograph shows a Panther G knocked out by the 2nd Armored's counterattack near Celles. (US National Archives)

A 'Big Red One' Sherman, from the US 1st Infantry Division, which was part of the force that held the Elsenborn Ridge and forced Model to change Sixth Panzer Army's mission. (US National Archives)

▶ *The 82nd Airborne held a 15-mile sector between the Germans and Liège. Over-extended, elements of its glider regiment were overrun at Baraque de Fraiture. Here men of the 325th Glider Regiment haul an ammunition sled through the snow-covered forest. (US National Archives)*

▼ *US M16 MGMC self-propelled anti-aircraft gun.*

net. Model ordered units forward to support the 2nd SS, but until they arrived he doubted the division's ability to continue.

Counterattack

When Montgomery took charge of the northern sector of the bulge, he demanded one particular American commander to support him: Major General Joseph 'Lightning Joe' Collins. Collins was the most able and aggressive American corps commander in Europe. Originally Montgomery wanted Collins's VII Corps held out of battle until it could deliver a massive counterstroke. But the German attack through Baraque de Fraiture had sucked the corps piecemeal into the defensive fighting. On the afternoon of 24 December, the commander of the 2nd Armored Division, Major General Ernest Harmon, phoned Collins's VII Corps headquarters to ask permission to attack the 2nd Panzer spearhead east of Dinant. Harmon had learned that the Germans were out of fuel and therefore vulnerable. Collins was absent, which led to a fortuitous command mix-up involving his subordinate and higher headquarters. The result was that Harmon believed he had won permission to prepare for an attack and so proceeded. When

Collins returned and learned of Harmon's plan, he decided to interpret Montgomery's and Hodges' restraining orders very broadly. He authorized an attack. On Christmas Day 2nd Armored Division advanced south-west from Ciney. Aided tremendously by Allied fighter-bombers, the crushing weight of American artillery and the panzers' lack of mobility owing to depleted fuel stocks, the division achieved spectacular results. It destroyed the 2nd Panzer's reconnaissance battalion and encircled the balance of the German force around Celles. The division destroyed or captured 82 tanks, 83 anti-tank and artillery pieces, 500 other assorted vehicles, and captured 1,213 men, while killing close to another 1,000. As had been Peiper's experience, the German division died at the point of its furthest penetration. The defeat of the 2nd Panzer Division forced the German High Command to re-evaluate all operations. The Germans had lost the initiative, although Hitler refused to accept this.

Command Crisis

The 2nd Armored Division's success brought into sharp relief the contrast between the American style of war and the Montgomery method. Two

◀After the fall of Baraque de Fraiture, the road to Liège briefly lay open. The Germans were unable to capitalize on this advantage, and soon tanks of the 3rd Armored Division had the route blocked. Here Shermans of 3rd Armored train their guns on the woods near Manhay. Narrow roads such as this one prevented all manoeuvre. (US National Archives)

▶ When Harmon learned that the 2nd Panzer had run out of fuel, he requested permission to attack. Here a Panther G, having run out of fuel, is captured by advancing Americans. (US National Archives)

▶ During the sixteen December days of the offensive, only five featured clear weather that permitted the Allies' full aerial arsenal to fly. Christmas Day was one clear day. The dreaded 'Jabos', fighter-bombers including ones like this P-47N, armed with eight .50-calibre machine-guns and two 1,000lb bombs or ten 5in rockets, joined the P-38 Lightnings and P-51 Mustangs to dominate ground combat. It was, according to the official historian, 'one of the greatest demonstrations of tactical ground support ever witnessed by American troops'. (US National Air & Space Museum)

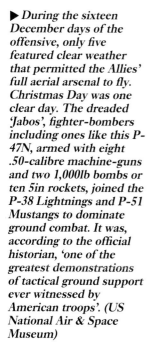

▶ Harmon's 2nd Armored Division captured much booty during its attack against the 2nd Panzer Division, such as these artillery pieces. (US National Archives)

① *Morning, 20 December: German 80-man patrol shot up by US AA half-tracks. Prisoners include officer from 2nd SS scouting advance routes for his division.*

DISTANCE FROM CROSSROADS TO FRAITURE : 1,000 YARDS

TO MANHAY

STONE WALL

TO SAMREE

② *Afternoon, 20 December: 'D' Troop, US 87th Cavalry squadron, joins defence; garrison ordered to 'hold as long as you can'.*

③ *German pressure builds around the crossroads, but lack of fuel delays attack. At dawn, 22 December, 2nd Battalion, US 325 Glider Infantry, garrisons Fraiture and sends its 'F' Company to the crossroads.*

④ *Night of 22 December: US tank-destroyer platoon sent to reinforce crossroads gets lost in the dark, halts and is captured by German infantry. The American position is now isolated.*

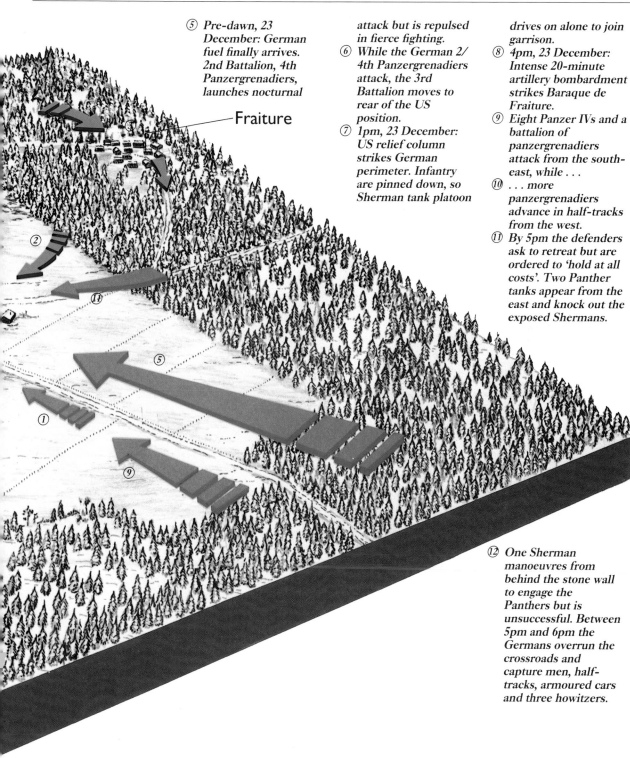

⑤ Pre-dawn, 23 December: German fuel finally arrives. 2nd Battalion, 4th Panzergrenadiers, launches nocturnal attack but is repulsed in fierce fighting.

⑥ While the German 2/4th Panzergrenadiers attack, the 3rd Battalion moves to rear of the US position.

⑦ 1pm, 23 December: US relief column strikes German perimeter. Infantry are pinned down, so Sherman tank platoon drives on alone to join garrison.

⑧ 4pm, 23 December: Intense 20-minute artillery bombardment strikes Baraque de Fraiture.

⑨ Eight Panzer IVs and a battalion of panzergrenadiers attack from the south-east, while . . .

⑩ . . . more panzergrenadiers advance in half-tracks from the west.

⑪ By 5pm the defenders ask to retreat but are ordered to 'hold at all costs'. Two Panther tanks appear from the east and knock out the exposed Shermans.

⑫ One Sherman manoeuvres from behind the stone wall to engage the Panthers but is unsuccessful. Between 5pm and 6pm the Germans overrun the crossroads and capture men, half-tracks, armoured cars and three howitzers.

COMBAT AT BARAQUE DE FRAITURE

20 to 23 December 1944.

days earlier Montgomery had decided to absorb another blow before counterattacking. He studied the maps and saw that the Germans had five panzer divisions lining the western and northern tip of the bulge, with additional major units hastening west. This convinced Montgomery that the Germans were about to deliver their most powerful blow since the first assault. The American commanders saw matters differently.

On the day Harmon smashed the 2nd Panzer Division, Bradley visited Montgomery. The Field Marshal lectured and scolded him like a schoolboy. He exaggerated the extent of the American setback, claiming Hodges' First Army would be unable to attack for three months. Later, in a letter to his British superior he wrote: 'It was useless to pretend that we were going to turn this quickly into a great victory; it was a proper defeat and we had better admit it.' He went on to say if his views had been followed all along this would not have happened.

In fact a great victory had been won. The offensive power of the German army had been smashed. 26 December, two days after Monty's lecture and letter, could be viewed as the high-water mark of the German offensive. While the GIs in the foxholes might not appreciate this fact, Bradley and Patton certainly did. Hodges' northern barrier from Dinant to Elsenborn stood firm. In the south, Bastogne had been relieved. The Americans felt that the over-extended German position invited a decisive counterstroke delivered from the shoulders of the bulge. They pointed to the 2nd Armored Division's success to support their view. Montgomery still adamantly disagreed. That night Bradley phoned Ike's chief of staff: 'Damn it, Bedell, can't you get Monty going in the north? As near as we can tell, the other fellow's reached the high-water mark today.'

This disagreement broadened into a serious rift that came close to fracturing the Anglo-American alliance. Recall that it was this fracture that Hitler had set as his goal when originally planning his 'master stroke'. Montgomery took advantage of the occasion to resume the strategic argument over a narrow versus broad advance into Germany. He used his temporary appointment as commander of American forces north of the bulge as a stepping stone toward his overall goal. On 30 December he baldly stated his demands in a letter to Eisenhower. He wrote that the Allies had just suffered a tremendous defeat. More would occur unless Ike acceded to his demand for 'one commander . . . to direct and control' all land operations in north-west Europe. He insisted that commander be himself.

For Eisenhower this was too much. He drafted a letter to the Combined Chiefs of Staff which presented the choice: Ike or Monty. Given the disparity in manpower, he knew Montgomery would go. Montgomery's dismissal would have enormous consequences. Promoted by an irresponsible press, virulent anti-American sentiment was sweeping England. Sacking Monty might mean an end to Anglo-American cooperation. Fortunately, into the breach stepped Montgomery's gifted chief of staff, Major General Francis de Guingand. After receiving a warning about what was afoot, de Guingand hurried to Eisenhower's headquarters. There the Supreme Commander's own chief of staff told him that it was too late: the decision had been made. Undaunted, de Guingand managed to persuade Eisenhower to delay any action for 24 hours. He returned to Montgomery and in one of the dramatic scenes of the war told his commander he was about to be sacked. The vain, confident Montgomery had no idea this was possible. He nearly collapsed and asked in a small voice: 'What do I do, Freddie?'

De Guingand had already written an abjectly apologetic letter. Monty signed it and sent it off. The letter concluded: 'Very distressed that my letter may have upset you and I would ask you to tear it up. Your very devoted subordinate, Monty.' This placated Eisenhower and the war went on.

▶ When US First and Third Armies cautiously attacked the tip of the Bulge, von Rundstedt ironically entered in the OB West War Diary 'the small solution'. Here tank crews of the Third Army take a cigarette break. Proud of his men, Patton issued Third Army a general order on 1 January: 'In closing, I can find no fitter expression for my feelings than to apply to you the immortal words spoken by General Scott at Chapultepec when he said, "Brave soldiers, veterans, you have been baptized in fire and blood and have come out steel."' (Charles B. MacDonald Collection, US Army Military History Institute)

CONCLUSION

Most of the generals on either side recognized 26 December as a turning point; henceforth the Americans held the initiative. Major combats remained. The German effort to again isolate Bastogne produced large-scale armoured actions. However, failure convinced von Manteuffel that it was time to retreat. Typically, Hitler proved slow to adjust to reality. Not until 8 January did he start Sixth Panzer Army moving east. When, on the Eastern Front, the tremendous Russian winter offensive struck four days later, the defenders lacked tanks and the front collapsed 'like a deck of cards'.

On 16 January, one month after the German assault, Patton's Third Army and Hodges' First Army linked up north-east of Bastogne. It was too

late to trap the mass of Germans. They had conducted a skilful fighting withdrawal under most difficult circumstances. Bradley proposed a 'hurry up offensive' to follow the Germans in hot pursuit through the Eifel and across the Rhine. This was a major departure from previous plans and proved unacceptable to Montgomery and too bold for Eisenhower. Yet ultimately the Rhine crossing at Remagen occurred precisely on this sector and featured the now veteran 9th Armored Division.

The Battle of the Bulge cost the American Army 10,276 killed, 47,493 wounded and a staggering 23,218 missing. German losses are impossible to quantify accurately. It is certain that their casualties exceeded the American total. The Germans lost hundreds of panzers. The Americans quickly replaced their losses. The Germans could not.

Assessment

The German armies never came close to achieving their objectives on the field in the Ardennes. However, according to Bradley, the German offensive caused high-level political and strategic battles that 'violently shook, and very nearly shattered, the Allied high command'. Such a rupture was exactly what Hitler intended. By this measure, 'Wacht am Rhein' came perilously close to success.

In modern war the one way high command can influence events once battle is joined is to allocate reserves. Accordingly, an evaluation of the top generals shows Eisenhower, and to a slightly lesser extent Bradley, to have performed exceedingly well in use of reserves to stop the German drive westwards. After the war, German generals commented that US reserves reacted more quickly than they had expected. Having accomplished this, Ike faltered by only partially following the recommendations of his subordinates – Bradley, Patton and Hodges – to cut off the Germans at the base of the bulge. Instead he pursued Montgomery's more cautious advance against the tip of the bulge. Had Montgomery been willing to use actively the British XXX Corps manning the Meuse to blunt the German advance, and thus use Collins to strike the Germans further east, Bradley writes: 'We could have inflicted an absolute slaughter on the Germans and, ultimately, saved many American lives.'

◄ *The frozen body of a German officer, one of thousands of Germans killed in the campaign. (US National Archives)*

Hitler and Jodl likewise failed to use their reserves wisely. Instead of exploiting Fifth Panzer Army's unexpected success, they reinforced Sixth Panzer Army's failure. By 20 December the German attack had escaped its generals' control. Why had the panzers failed to advance as planned?

The ability of most Americans to stand firm in the face of surprise assault vitally influenced events. The stubborn initial defence disrupted the OKW's carefully prepared plans. It bought enough time for American resistance to harden along more organized defensive lines. With each passing day, coordinated resistance in a region with limited roads made the German task of reaching the Meuse less feasible. It is important to note that merely reaching the Meuse was only the first objective in the plan to capture Antwerp. German tactical support and logistics failed to keep pace with the advance. As early as 19 December, Fifth Panzer Army reported a 'badly strained' fuel supply. The next day the Sixth's 12th SS Panzer Division, supposedly a spearhead unit, ground to a halt for lack of fuel. OKW bungled badly when it failed to ensure that fuel distribution keep pace with the advance, when it miscalculated fuel

expenditures – bad terrain and weather reduced the expected mileage from a tankful of fuel by fifty per cent – and when it optimistically based spearhead advances on captured stocks.

The US Army in the Ardennes Campaign did not serve its soldiers well. It equipped the GI with inferior weapons, trained and organized him according to a faulty doctrine, allowed the enemy to launch a massive surprise offensive against his weakest point and frequently provided poor leadership at army, corps and divisional levels. By and large the American soldier returned valour. Some ran at first shock; most stood firm and fought with what they had.

In his post-war interrogation, von Manteuffel acknowledged the success of the American delaying action. But he proudly noted that 2nd Panzer Division spearheads reached to within four kilometres of the Meuse without a major engagement. While this is true, the division accomplished this feat only at the expense of bypassing all defended positions and leaving it up to supporting units to carve a supply route. Von Manteuffel believed that the second wave's failure was inherent in the original plan. The Germans lacked the strength to

◀ *Two very young Waffen SS troopers captured during the American advance to erase the Bulge. (Charles B. MacDonald Collection, US Army Military History Institute)*

feed the offensive and enough strength to capture the positions bypassed by the first assault wave.

Von Manteuffel also observed that the German High Command failed to convert to the 'small solution' when it became apparent that the all-out drive to Antwerp was impracticable. This observation does raise a most interesting 'what if'? Ridgeway's XVII Airborne Corps' defences facing south were spread exceedingly thinly during the days it focused on screening the withdrawal from St Vith. As late as the fall of Manhay on 24 December, German armour had the opportunity to slice in behind the forces concentrated around St Vith and on the Elsenborn Ridge. They could have trapped this force in a vice, using the Meuse as a barrier, and inflicted a very serious defeat. What impact such a defeat would have had on the Eisenhower-Montgomery feud is difficult to assess, but it is interesting to note that Eisenhower challenged Montgomery knowing that his own standing with the American government was secure. In the event, the partial victory obtainable from the 'small solution' was not in keeping with Hitler's aims. He sought overwhelming victory and was incapable of realizing that his means did not match his hopes. For, in the last analysis, from its inception the German Ardennes offensive had no reasonable chance of victory.

Before their execution Field Marshals Jodl and Keitel responded to a question about the wisdom of the Ardennes offensive: 'The criticism whether it would have been better to have employed our available reserves in the East rather than in the West, we submit to the judgment of history.' Given that the attack had slight chance of success but did limit Anglo-American penetration east by the end of the war, it can be asserted that one effect of the offensive was to place more Germans and other Europeans under Russian rather than Western occupation after the cessation of hostilities.

Winston Churchill paid eloquent tribute to the American forces in a speech before the House of Commons on 18 January 1945. He concluded that the Battle of the Bulge was 'undoubtedly the greatest American battle of the War, and will, I believe, be regarded as an ever-famous American victory.'

The inscription beneath a statue of a GI in the town of Clervaux, the site of the 110/28 Division's last stand against von Manteuffel's panzers, reminds modern tourists what the American sacrifice and victory meant. It reads: 'To Our Liberators.'

◄ *Guarded by a GI of the 4th Armored Division, captured Germans assist their comrade, suffering from frostbite, to the rear. (US Army Military History Institute)*

THE BATTLEFIELD TODAY

The area is large and the actions were many. Therefore, I recommend selecting a centrally located touring base such as Clervaux. The now-serene castle houses a Battle of the Bulge Museum well worth a visit. Americans will feel welcome in this village, especially when they come upon the memorial to American soldiers.

The Hotel du Parc overlooking Clervaux, and the Vieux Moulin d'Åsselborn near the village of Asselborn a few kilometres away, offer quiet lodgings at a reasonable price and excellent food. In the guest-book at the latter inn we saw the names of 101st Airborne veterans.

From either of these bases, one can conveniently visit Bastogne to the south-west and its Battle of the Bulge Museum, or hunt for foxholes and memorials among the woods and villages to the north and east. Foxholes with both German

and American relics can be found in a pine wood outside Rocherath-Krinkelt. In villages across the front, such as Echternach, Houffalize and Stavelot, there are preserved German or American tanks. At the edge of a quiet road through a wood outside Meyerode is a memorial to Lieutenant Eric Fisher Wood, an American reputed to have conducted a series of guerrilla actions in the area before he was killed. Here too people remember; on a rainy late-September day, I found fresh cut flowers at the foot of the memorial.

▼ *The 7th Armored Division passes three German tanks on 23 January as it drives to re-enter St Vith. (US Army Military History Institute)*

CHRONOLOGY

1944

6 June D-Day, the Allied invasion of France.
25 July Allied breakout from beachhead begins.
19 August Hitler initiates planning to assemble reserves for counteroffensive in the West.
Early September Allied pursuit across Europe grinds to a halt owing to supply shortages.
10 September US First Army liberates Luxemburg.
16 September Hitler announces intention to launch counteroffensive through Ardennes. Objective: Antwerp.
20 September Soviet forces cross the River Danube.
25 September Montgomery's Operation 'Market Garden' ends in failure.
1 October First Army begins siege of Aachen; Montgomery begins Scheldt campaign to clear Antwerp approaches.
Late October Russians attack into East Prussia.
8 November US Third Army begins drive to breach the German West Wall defence line.
16 November US First Army begins Huertgen Forest campaign.
28 November First Allied ships reach Antwerp; long period of Allied supply shortage eases.
13 December US First Army launches attack to capture River Roer dams; Germans mass in forward staging areas.
16 December, 5.30am Germans open all-out counteroffensive in Ardennes.
Daytime Losheim Gap defences begin to crumble. Sixth Panzer Army assault stalls against US 2nd and 99th Divisions. Fifth Panzer Army makes limited progress against 28th Division.
Night Losheim Gap position crumbles; 106th Division on verge of being surrounded. 110/28 positions fall to German armour. Eisenhower releases 7th and 10th Armored Divisions from reserve.

17 December
Morning Peiper captures Bullingen; 18th VGD captures Schoenberg bridge, isolating US 106th Division.
Afternoon Peiper's SS slaughter unarmed Americans near Malmédy; traffic jams delay German advance on St Vith.
Night Peiper halts before Stavelot; Eisenhower releases airborne divisions.
18 December Peiper repulsed at Trois Ponts; US armour delays German advance on Bastogne.
19 December
Morning 101st checks Panzer Lehr outside Bastogne; Peiper isolated by recapture of Stavelot.
Afternoon 7,000-8,000 American troops surrender on Schnee Eifel; defence of St Vith stiffens.
Night Eisenhower convenes emergency meeting.
20 December Montgomery assumes command of US First Army.
21 December St Vith falls.
22 December McAuliffe rejects surrender demand; Bastogne low on ammunition.
Night St Vith defenders retreat from salient.
23 December Peiper retreats with remnant on foot; defenders of Bastogne re-supplied by air; 2nd SS Division captures Baraque de Fraiture.
25 December Major attack on Bastogne repulsed; 2nd Panzer Division spearhead mauled 4 kilometres short of Meuse; von Rundstedt requests abandoning 'Wacht am Rhein' and substituting the 'small solution'.
26 December US 4th Armored Division relieves Bastogne; initiative passes into Allies' hands.
29 December Allied 'crisis in command' begins with Montgomery's letter to Eisenhower requesting new command arrangement.
30 December Last German effort to close Bastogne corridor fails; von Manteuffel abandons hope for offensive action.

1945

1 January Luftwaffe launches 'Great Blow' in West and suffers irreplaceable losses of nearly 300 aircraft.

8 January Hitler authorizes SS withdrawal from Ardennes.

12 January Soviets begin massive winter offensive across River Vistula in Poland.

16 January US First and Third Armies join at Houffalize.

23 January US CCB/7 Armored Division re-enters St Vith.

28 January Battle of the Bulge officially ends.

7 March US First Army seizes Remagen bridge across River Rhine.

23 March Allied forces under Montgomery cross Rhine north of the Ruhr.

1 April US First and Ninth Armies encircle the Ruhr.

23 April Soviet forces break into Berlin.

25 April US and Soviet patrols meet on either side of River Elbe.

30 April Hitler commits suicide in Berlin.

7 May German High Command unconditionally surrenders all forces.

A GUIDE TO FURTHER READING

BLUMENSON, M. *The Patton Papers 1940-1945*, (vol. 2) Boston, 1974. Patton's diary, revealing his thinking at the time.

BRADLEY, O. and BLAIR, C. *A General's Life*, New York, 1983. Much about grand strategy and the Montgomery feud.

COLE, H. *The Ardennes: Battle of the Bulge*, Washington, 1965. The indispensable official history, but written before declassification of Ultra.

EUROPEAN THEATER HISTORICAL INTERROGATION, Series A Manuscripts 1945; Series B 1946-48, National Archives, Washington. Of particular interest are A872 for OB information, B151 for planning and preparation; and B151A for von Manteuffel's detailed description and critique.

GILES, J. *The Damned Engineers*, Washington, 1985. A detailed account of the engineers' role in delaying the German offensive. Special focus on Peiper's advance.

GOOLRICK, W. and TANNER, O. *The Battle of the Bulge*, Alexandria, VA, 1979. Lavishly illustrated, good general account.

MacDONALD, C. *A Time for Trumpets: The Untold Story of the Battle of the Bulge*, New York, 1985. A recent, exhaustively detailed account. Examines in detail what the Allies knew before the attack.

— *Company Commander*, Washington, 1947. What it was like at the sharp end in front of the twin villages on 17 December.

MARSHALL, S. *Bastogne: The Story of the First Eight Days*, Washington, 1946. Based on combat interviews shortly after battle.

PIMLOTT, J. *Battle of the Bulge*, New York, 1981. An overview with sharp analysis.

WARLIMONT, W. *Inside Hitler's Headquarters 1939-45*, New York, 1964. The view from within by a professional staff officer who was there.

WEIGLEY, R. *Eisenhower's Lieutenants: The Campaign of France and Germany 1944-1945*, Bloomington, IN, 1981. Focuses on leadership and command decisions. Excellent analysis of US Army's weaknesses.

WARGAMING ARDENNES 1944

The German counter-offensive in the Ardennes was a massive operation which eventually involved a large number of divisions battling for a salient some sixty miles deep. With this scale of conflict (unfortunately common in the twentieth century) wargamers hoping to re-create military action need to consider which aspect or aspects of the battle most interest them and then select the most appropriate 'level' and form of wargame for their purposes. To assist in this choice, the following suggestions for wargaming Operation 'Wacht am Rhein' and its resulting battles are divided into two categories: first, the operational level or 'High Command'; and second, the tactical approach, 'The Sharp End'.

High Command

If the responsibilities of a five-star general or *generalfeldmarschall* rest easily on your shoulders then the obvious approach to the 'Battle of the Bulge' is to attempt the whole thing – albeit in a greatly scaled-down form. Taking on the mantle of an army group commander seems an awesome prospect, bearing in mind the logistic complexities of mechanized warfare, but such concerns can be eased by the purchase of a commercial boardgame – the kind of boxed game pioneered by manufacturers such as Avalon Hill and found on the shelves of most hobby and model shops. These games are self-contained and often lavishly presented, their main drawbacks being the complexity of some of the rulebooks (although after gaining experience with the simpler games these usually present less of a problem) and availability. The games that are relevant to our search for the 'High Command' view of the Ardennes counter-offensive include: *Battle of the Bulge, Hitler's Last Gamble, Bastogne* and *Battles for the Ardennes*. The first-mentioned has been the 'standard' Ardennes

game for many years now, and because of its age it is relatively cheap. Nevertheless, it still appears regularly in the boardgames charts – a sure sign of its playability. The last-mentioned game is a 'quad' (a four-game package on a common theme), which includes three games relevant to the 1944/5 conflict; but, alas, the manufacturer is now defunct and its availability is unknown. The best course of action in the event of your local shop failing to 'come up with the goods' is to contact the manufacturers direct. All the major wargaming magazines carry advertisements for these companies or mail order outlets who stock their products – some of the latter specializing in games that are now discontinued.

Although these games give relatively accurate and detailed pictures of the problems facing commanders on both sides, my personal feeling is that they tend to lack 'soul'. If a straightforward game is all you desire, then fine. However, the question of High Command (as this book clearly shows) goes beyond logistic and strategic concerns and often strays into the realms of personal aims, military rivalries and political diplomacy. Boardgames can, of course, be adapted to introduce some of these factors. Playing with several players on each side, for example, will not only begin to introduce the feel of a chain of command but also superimpose the personalities of the players on to the cardboard counters they control. Many boxed games of the sort described above are intended for multi-player use, and with enough players involved a military hierarchy can be produced that distances the most senior officers from the detailed minutiae of brigade and even divisional movements.

The next stage is physically to remove the players from the gaming table and set up command headquarters behind screens or in different rooms. With one (or several) umpires now given the task of controlling the movement of pieces on the map board, the American and German players begin to experience more fully the problems and frustrations of command; their decisions having to be based on incomplete, or even contradictory, intelligence reports fed to them by the umpires, or by subordinates allowed a limited glimpse of their sector of the main battle map. With the pressure on – aided by a fixed time for each game move – the 'High Command' may soon find themselves at odds over where to send the vital American reserves, or how best to accelerate the faltering SS panzer thrust in the north.

If the number of players is sufficient and the 'layer cake' of command sufficiently deep, then this may also be the best way to simulate an essentially tactical problem that nevertheless influenced the strategic responses of all American units: the operations of the German commando units disguised as American troops. To re-create the effects of this small-scale, but highly effective, piece of military subterfuge umpires will have to be given sufficient leeway to produce unexpected US hold-ups and diversions – perhaps even some limited acts of sabotage. If this is done skilfully – bearing in mind the advantage of hindsight that any historically aware player will bring to his role – the American commanders may be forced into the near paranoic reactions to the threat of 'fifth columnists' that in December 1944 engendered fears of Eisenhower being abducted and of every non-baseball fan being a German spy.

It may be that, inspired by such a game, the player, or players, decide to devise their own strategic simulation – researching the subject from books such as this and, in the process, learning far more about what made men like Brigadier General Anthony ('Nuts') McAuliffe and General Hasso von Manteuffel tick. The great advantage of a 'homespun' game is that it can be tailored to your personal interests – emphasizing the aspect of the battle that you find most fascinating. In addition, the rules can be written as simply or with as much complexity as you desire – certainly they are unlikely to require the quasi-legal jargon found in some professionally produced boardgame rules (unless, of course, you cannot trust your regular opponents). Game mechanisms are normally simple beasts, and even the professionals 'borrow'

each other's ideas with regularity, so would-be game designers should not be afraid of attempting a synthesis that suits them and their particular view of the Ardennes conflict. There is also the additional satisfaction of producing your own map (or purchasing a hex-printed overlay to convert your tourist guide of the area) and counters – the professional versions of the latter all too frequently being utilitarian and uninspiring.

Another approach to the whole business of 'High Command' is to shed the rule-book completely and embark on what is termed a 'committee game' – essentially a role-playing simulation of planning meetings, or crucial gatherings of 'top brass' to shape strategic responses. This is undoubtedly the best way of 'gaming' such aspects of the Ardennes battles as the preliminary planning of the German attack. Players taking the parts of von Rundstedt and Model can be set the task of arguing for more modest goals than the re-capture of Antwerp, while Hitler and his cronies promote the Führer's ambitious plan to split the Allied forces, deny their source of supplies and send them packing across the Channel. A game of this nature does not require histrionic amateur dramatics, but should give players a clear indication of their personal aims and general demeanour. Research will again benefit realism in both the facts and figures presented and the arguments they support.

For crushingly obvious outcomes, such as the Allied commanders' reaction to reports of a German build-up in the Eifel (assuming they have all just read this book!), it would be wise to adopt a 'disguised scenario', a technique devised by British wargamer Arthur Harman. In this case the Ardennes may become a fictitious wooded sector of the Russian Front in late 1941 – the victorious 'Allies' being represented by German and Axis forces, the build-up consisting of Russian infantry and precious reserves of T-34s and KV-1s. By keeping players in the dark about the true nature of the scenario, their reactions to similar reports coming from a 'quiet', 'impassable' sector may be instructive.

Finally, there is possibly no other way than the commitee game of adequately contesting the political ramifications of this particular battle, notably General De Gaulle's strong resistance to Eisenhower's transfer of Patton's forces from the hard-won and vulnerable Alsace region to the threatened north. Once again, research is the key. Coupled with a clear understanding of each individual's personal goals (kept secret from other players and ultimately assessed on an agreed scale of 'points'), a game of this nature can give the most direct insight into the senior commander's world.

Strategic games such as those above can also be linked with the more traditional approach of using model vehicles and figures to represent the opposing forces. Although miniatures are inappropriate for the fighting of large-scale actions in the twentieth century, they can be used to game the smaller clashes that result from strategic map moves – a common practice when fighting campaigns in other historical periods. The American 'Command Decision' rules and scenarios for the Second World War combine elements of both methods by scaling model forces down to manageable proportions (1:5 for vehicles, a 'stand' of 2 figures representing a platoon), thus enabling higher formations to 'fight it out' on the table top after preliminary map manoeuvres and by laying emphasis on the decision-making of company commanders and above. More specifically, there is a 'Command Decision' scenario in booklet form that deals in detail with the battle for Bastogne. Called simply *Bastogne*, it gives detailed scaled-down organization tables for the forces involved and all other relevant material (bar the rules themselves) for gaming this epic of American defence, using 1/76th or 1/300th scale model soldiers and vehicles. This game devolves down to small-unit actions and provides a logical link to the second part of this guide to wargaming the 'Battle of the Bulge', the tactical approach.

'The Sharp End'

One of the most interesting wargaming developments in recent years has been the upsurge in games and game systems that deal with the experiences of small units – the squads, platoons and single tanks that figured so prominently in the desperate fighting for supremacy in the Ardennes. For gamers so inclined, there are several boxed boardgames that (at a price) offer highly detailed scenarios in a well-researched and well-presented package. These include *Squad Leader, Advanced Squad Leader, Soldier* and *Ambush*, the latter being a solitaire or single-player game. For a taste of individual tank warfare, *Patton's Best* is based upon the day-to-day ordeals of a single vehicle in the 4th Armoured Division. The emphasis in most of these games is on leadership and motivation – based on the Second World War research of pioneering US battlefield historian S. L. A. Marshall, who discovered that most infantrymen are not natural fighters and need a lot of encouragement to risk their skins in an advance or fire-fight. The disadvantages of such games lie only in the non-specifically 'Ardennes-orientated' nature of some of the scenarios and the cost involved in purchasing all the necessary modules. For example, the tremendously popular *Advanced Squad Leader* game system boasts an all-American module entitled 'Yanks', giving counters representing all conceivable types of US Army troops, their weapons, supporting tanks, guns and vehicles. Out of the eight scenarios offered in this module are two concerning German panzer-grenadier attacks in the Ardennes. To play these scenarios the gamer needs to have purchased *Advanced Squad Leader* and another module, *Beyond Valor*.

Popular and well-presented as these games are, perhaps more satisfying (and cheaper) is the research and modelling of small units that can be used to re-fight some of the many 'minor' actions that erupted as German spearheads tried to force their passage to the west. With miniatures, the wargamer has a variety of scales to choose from: the diminutive 1/300th (6mm) offering the largest battlefield per table inches; 1/200th adding more 'bulk' to the armour and figures; and the increasingly resurgent 1/76th scale, which sacrifices battle space for detail and aesthetic appeal. Many sets of rules exist for Second World War warfare in all three scales and should be found to be suitable for the Ardennes if appropriate measures are taken to allow for narrow, twisting and often muddy roads; the appalling weather conditions; and the resulting lack of air support for much of the battle.

Several aspects of the tactical 'Battle of the Bulge' lend themselves to representation in miniature, one of the more unusual being Operation 'Greif' and the actions of Otto Skorzeny's Panzerbrigade 150. The clash near Malmédy between Skorkenzy's five Panthers disguised as US M10 tank destroyers and a handful of the genuine article saw company-sized units of infantry engaged in a desperate struggle for a vital river crossing, the fighting pivoting around a single house held by a tank destroyer platoon headquarters, some engineers and a few infantry – 30 men all told.

This was an action that featured one of the first uses of the Allies' new proximity-fuzed artillery shells, a weapon developed for use by anti-aircraft units initially and then stockpiled as an emergency measure in case of a major German counter-attack. The unexpected effects of shells that burst in the air rather than on the ground should be taken into account when calculating German morale if under fire from US artillery. Yet another aspect of this eventful skirmish was the Congressional Medal of Honor winning tank-stalking of Private Francis Currey, who carried out a series of heroic feats, including taking on three Panthers single-handed. This is an element of the conflict that could be re-created using one-figure-represents-one-man skirmish rules. These allow for details of activity such as loading weapons, crawling, wounds to different parts of the body and differing skill levels.

Although there appears to be a degree of misguided 'glamour' attached to SS units (whether due to their 'élite' status or possession of the more exotic armoured hardware it is hard to say; events at Malmédy should remind wargamers of their inherent unpleasantness), the actions of von Manteuffel's more successful Wehrmacht divisions, and the *ersatz* Volksgrenadier units, offer more opportunities for varied scenarios.

Bastogne has been mentioned, but other less permanent holding actions, such as that carried out by the 10th Armored Division on the approaches to the town, or the defence of St Vith by 7th Armored, could form the basis for games where the American objective is to delay rather than defeat the enemy.

For those who tire of endless tank confrontations, the attacks by Brandenberger's Seventh Army pit the low strength and lightly equipped Volksgrenadier divisions against surprised US troops holding lines too extensive for their resources. Rules for movement in snow and the varying resolution of isolated pockets of American troops should be introduced to give the right 'feel' to these actions.

Finally, the activities of the German 'fire brigade', the Paratroop divisions, provide numerous opportunities for interesting games. The abortive paratroop drop to the north of the 'Bulge' could be re-created, or the actions of small 'independent' groups of paratroops who hitched lifts on SS panzers, acting as close support when resistance was encountered.

As a guide to wargaming a major battle of the Second World War, this chapter is necessarily brief and relatively general. One can only hope that it encourages the newcomer to wargaming and inspires a few 'old hands' who have steered clear of what they might have regarded as a 'tank scrum'. At this juncture a few points vital to the 'flavour' of the Ardennes conflict may perhaps be suggested.

Terrain is often sadly neglected in miniatures wargaming, and with the 'Battle of the Bulge' we have an action in which it cannot be ignored. The creation of model railway style scenery may not necessarily be the answer, but certainly some attempt at relief is vital, as it both obscured and channelled the German advance – the frequent mention of 'hair-pin' bends and 'deep ravines' in contemporary accounts indicating that the natural features of the Ardennes made a strong impression on soldiers of both sides.

Weather is similarly neglected in many games, but any re-creation of the 'Bulge' must take into consideration mist, snow and low cloud, which affected visibility, movement rates and air cover respectively. The latter was, of course, an essential element of the German plan, and the crucial break in the overcast conditions will decide when US fighter-bombers can wreak havoc among the panzer columns and when the defenders of Bastogne can be re-supplied from the air.

The nature of the roads in the Ardennes, the few serviceable bridges and the ever-pervading mud led to enormous traffic jams during the German advance, particularly in the north. Such clutters of vehicles are all too frequently seen in tank *v.* tank 'football matches', when both players try to use too many of the heaviest armour possible; but a game posing the problem of effectively routeing advancing (or retreating) motorized columns – especially under fire or imminent air attack – could give purpose to the military police figures now found in a number of miniatures ranges.

Finally, a word on tanks – the vital ingredient of the German assault. The heavy armour of the late war period can be both an attraction and a marked disadvantage to gaming this battle. It is interesting to note that German spearheads were frequently led by infantry, or tanks in single file, and that Joachim Peiper relegated his inherited King Tigers – the heaviest tank available on either side – to the rear of his column to prevent them slowing his advance.

Wargames in boxes, miniature vehicles, aircraft, figures and terrain (including scenic terrain sections) are now available in a bewildering array of scales and materials. A visit to your local specialist hobby shop, or a flick through the pages of wargames magazines such as *Wargames Illustrated*, will provide the items you need to refight the 'Battle of the Bulge'. The latter will also inform you about current wargames thinking and inspire aspirant painters with some superb colour photographs.

Colour figure illustrators:
Cilla Eurich, pages 10 and 14; Angus McBride, page 22; David Parker and Ron Volstad, pages 18, 19, 30, 46, 51 and 54; Steven J. Zaloga, pages 43 and 79.